portrait of ireland

Ireland~Past and Present

portrait of
ireland

Ireland~Past and Present
LIAM DE PAOR

ST. MARTIN'S PRESS
NEW YORK

3

ST. MARTIN'S PRESS

Library of Congress Cataloging-in-Publication Data

De Paor, Liam.
  Portrait of Ireland.

  1. Ireland — Civilization.   I. Title.
DA925.D39 1985   941.5   85-27829

ISBN 0-312-63180-4

Conceptual design by Liam Miller
First published in Ireland by Rainbow Publications, Ltd.
First U.S. Edition

By the same author.

Early Christian Ireland (M. De Paor) published in U.S.A.

Rainbow Publications wishes to gratefully acknowledge contributions from the following for the illustration of this book:

Tomb chamber, Knowth, Co. Meath © courtesy of the Commissioners of Public Works, Dublin

Megalithic Tomb Carrowmore, Co. Sligo © courtesy of the Commissioners of Public Works, Dublin.

Athgreany stone circle, Co. Wicklow © courtesy of the Commissioners of Public Works, Dublin

Knocknarea, Co. Sligo © courtesy of Bord Fáilte, Dublin

Manuscript page from the Book of Leinster © courtesy of Trinity College, Dublin

Turoe stone, Co. Galway © courtesy of the Commissioners of Public Works, Dublin

Kildare St. Brigid's cross © courtesy of the National Museum, Dublin

Aerial view of Tara, Co. Meath © courtesy of the Commissioners of Public Works, Dublin

"Mound of The Hostages" © courtesy of Bord Fáilte, Dublin.

Reproduction of St. Manchan's Shrine © courtesy of the National Museum, Dublin

Excavations at Wood Quay © courtesy of The Irish Times

View of Trinity College by James Malton © courtesy of the National Gallery of Ireland

Statue of Edmund Burke. Trinity College © courtesy of Bord Fáilte, Dublin

Civic offices, Wood Quay © courtesy of The Irish Times

Interior of a Nineteenth Century Country Inn © courtesy of The National Library Dublin

Old Abbey Theatre © courtesy of The Abbey Theatre, Dublin

Joyce's Tower, Sandycove, Co. Dublin © courtesy of Bord Fáilte, Dublin

Statue of George Bernard Shaw © courtesy of the National Gallery, of Ireland

Samuel Beckett © courtesy of The Irish Times

Seán Ó Faoláin © courtesy of The Irish Times

Portrait of Seamus Heaney by Edward Maguire © courtesy of the Ulster Museum, Belfast and by kind permission the artist

DART train © courtesy of Coras Janpair Eireann
Portrait of W.B. Yeats © courtesy of The National Library Dublin and by kind permission of Mr. Michael Yeats

Dublin after Bord Fáilte, 1985 © courtesy of Bord Fáilte
Liam de Paor © courtesy of The Irish Times
National Stud, Co. Kildare © courtesy of Bord Fáilte, Dublin
Ferbane power station, Co. Offaly © courtesy of the Electricity Supply Board
Guinness brewery, Dublin © courtesy of Guinness Group Sales, Dublin
Clew Bay, Co. Mayo © courtesy of Bord Fáilte, Dublin
Clonmacnoise, Co. Offaly © courtesy of Bord Fáilte, Dublin
Giant's Causeway, Co. Antrim © courtesy of the Northern Ireland Tourist Board
Florencecourt, Co. Fermanagh © courtesy of the Northern Ireland Tourist Board
Great Skellig, Co. Kerry © courtesy of Bord Fáilte, Dublin
Armagh © courtesy of the Northern Ireland Tourist Board
O'Connell monument, Glasnevin © courtesy of Bord Fáilte, Dublin
Statue of James Larkin, O'Connell Street © courtesy of Bord Fáilte, Dublin
Kilkenny © courtesy of Bord Fáilte, Dublin
Dunluce Castle, Co. Antrim © courtesy of the Northern Ireland Tourist Board
Belfast City Hall © courtesy of the Northern Ireland Tourist Board
Belfast Academical Institution © courtesy of the Northern Ireland Tourist Board
Fleadh Cheoil, Co. Donegal © courtesy of Bord Fáilte, Dublin
Steeple chasing, Co. Kilkenny © courtesy of Bord Fáilte, Dublin
Hurling in Croke Park, Dublin © courtesy of Bord Fáilte, Dublin
Irish Soldiers on UNIFIL Duty in Lebanon © courtesy of The National Library Dublin
Book of Kells © courtesy of Trinity College, Dublin
Bourne Vincent Memorial Park © courtesy of the Commissioners of Public Works, Dublin
Stormont, Belfast © courtesy of the Northern Ireland Tourist Board
Dublin Airport © courtesy of Aer Lingus Publicity Department
The Docks, Galway © courtesy of Bord Fáilte, Dublin
Cliffs of Inishmore, Aran © courtesy of the Commissioners of Public Works, Dublin
"Cross of The Scriptures", Clonmacnoise, © courtesy of the Commissioners of Public Works, Dublin.

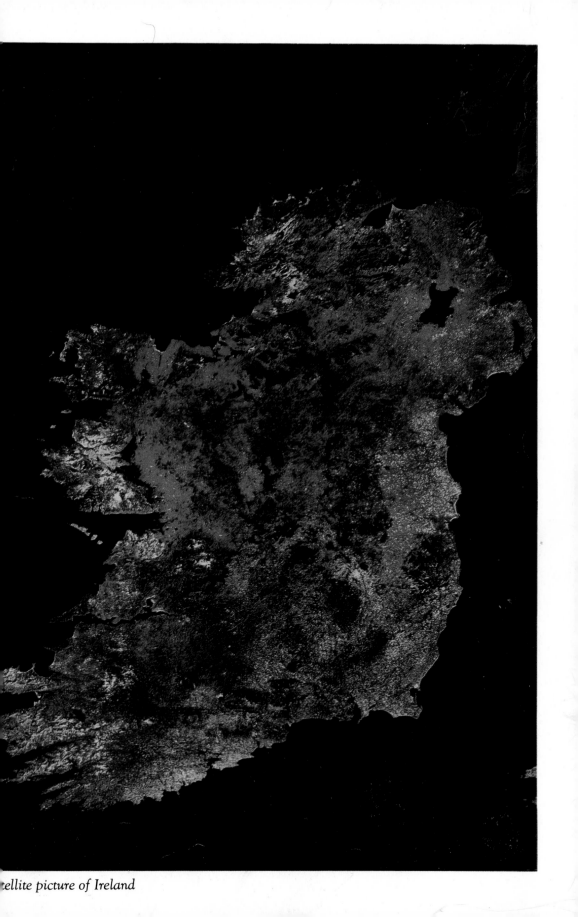

Satellite picture of Ireland

Joyce's Tower, Sandycove, Co. Dublin

Mare and foals grazing at the National Stud, Co. Kildare

Gateway to Guinness brewery in Dublin

Ferbane Power Station, Co. Offaly

CONTENTS

FOREWORD

A Portrait of Ireland is just that. It is a look at the country through the eyes of one person, and an attempt to delineate not so much its superficial features as something of the underlying character.

A country, however, is not a person. A country indeed, in most of the ways in which we use a word like 'Ireland', is an abstraction. We are using shorthand, or a cipher, to refer to a complex system of shifting composition and meaning. But there does exist a concrete piece of rock and soil, surrounded by the North Atlantic and its lesser seas, and inhabited by some five million concrete living and breathing people at the present day. With a selection of generalisations we can try to discuss the people on their island, and those who went before them, in ways that will have some approximation to truth.

For the greater part of the 1970s I wrote a regular column in the *Irish Times* under the general title, 'Roots'. It ranged fairly widely in subject matter but was, broadly, an exploration of the relationship between past and present in Ireland. Through it I looked at various aspects of Irish culture — in the anthropological, as well as narrower senses of that somewhat ambiguous word. An early training in architecture and archaeology developed in me the habit of trying to understand people through the things they have made, both for utility and for those other, mysterious, aesthetic reasons which are never absent, I believe, from the intention of the person fashioning even the simplest and humblest of utensils. The emphases in 'Roots' reflected these preoccupations, and it was very often through looking at physical or cultural artefacts that I tried to understand some of the complexities of our present as well as our past. In this short book I have drawn on some passages from those occasional writings of the seventies, where they were expressing ideas or thoughts about Ireland that I have held for some time. But this is mainly a re-thinking of those ideas.

For a number of years now, Ireland has been known to many people in the world — very dimly, probably, to most of them — largely as one of the world's trouble-spots. The nature of the trouble has been both simplified and falsified by the casual background-sketches of the reporters and anchor-persons in Toronto, Newcastle-upon-Tyne or Munich who break a three-month silence on Ireland to report a bomb or a riot, with a twenty-second film clip. A religious war, or 'mindless' terrorism, are two of the standard, if not very intelligible, interpretations offered. Our global village is such that nowadays a large part of the people of the Republic of Ireland are just as baffled — and horrified — by what happens in Northern Ireland as are people much farther away. In Northern Ireland itself there is more understanding as well as more prejudice.

But this book is not about Northern Ireland nor about Ireland as one of the fever-spots of a troubled world. In the middle decades of this century Ireland was relatively crime-free and the general incidence of violence was low. It is still, even with the conflict in Northern Ireland, less violent than many other places. More people are killed or maimed on the roads in car-accidents than by bombs or guns. More people are killed by bombs or guns in Dallas, Detroit and New York than in Northern Ireland — and cars kill people there too. (The car-deaths are not a wholly unfair comparison. This is a choice made by society — to accept on the roads what a British spokesman in a different context called 'an acceptable level of violence' rather than undergo a certain amount of inconvenience.) The conflict is, in fact, muted so far. There is always a possibility that it might become much more unrestrained, but up to the time of writing it is by no means so overwhelming in its general effects that there is nothing else to be said about Ireland.

Although Ireland is a small not very densely populated island, it has in the past produced a distinctive civilisation and, in comparatively recent times, considerable contributions to literature and thought. It has a comparatively 'high profile'. From the island such large numbers have gone to settle overseas that Ireland must be considered a mother country of some significance. About a fifth of the population of the United States of America fairly recently signified 'Irish' as their ethnic origin, and there are many in other parts of the world who would admit some connection, near or distant, with the country. Yet, what its contributions to the world have been is not well known. This book does not attempt to expound them; but it does try to depict Ireland itself, briefly, impressionistically, and, as far as possible, objectively.

Dublin 1985

1
LANDSCAPES

'The mountains', wrote the great French historian Fernand Braudel, 'are as a rule a world apart from civilizations, which are an urban and a lowland achievement. Their history is to have none, to remain almost always on the fringe of the great waves of civilization, even the longest and most persistent, which may spread over great distances on the horizontal plane but are powerless to move vertically when faced with an obstacle of a few hundred metres'.

Here is the key to Ireland. Braudel was writing, with love, learning and intimate knowledge, of the Mediterranean sea and the complex peninsulas which rim it and intersect it, each springing from an intercourse of mountain and plain. His history begins with and is founded on the shapes of the lands, the mould within which his 'waves of civilization', along with other human manifestations, have ebbed and flowed. Ireland, in its spatial relations with the surrounding ocean, with the archipelago of which it is a part, and with the nearby mainland of Europe, is equally complex.

It too is compounded of mountain and plain, intimately related. In a mere 85,000 square kilometres there is remarkable variety of landscape. The coast is deeply fretted with innumerable bays and inlets, the interior mysteriously interwoven with winding streams and countless bogs and lakes among the pastures and the farms. No mountains are high — there are few points more than a thousand metres above sea-level — yet in Ireland too 'an obstacle of a few hundred metres' or even less can have an effect enduring for hundreds or thousands of years.

Take, more or less at random, a viewpoint in the middling parts of the island. The town of Carlow, within the south-eastern quarter of Ireland, is on the Barrow, a small river which flows due south to enter the sea through the long estuary of Waterford Harbour. Behind Carlow to the east the lonely hills and valleys of Wicklow cut the town off, firmly and finally, from the Irish Sea. To the west, just two or three kilometres beyond the river, is an escarpment. The ground simply lifts suddenly from the plain of the river valley — not very much but very noticeably. It is a ledge, and the skyline to the west is the monotonous profile of a low plateau. The roads that cross the Barrow rise steeply for a few hundred metres on the escarpment, and as they do so the landscape changes abruptly. At Carlow itself, in the centre of the town, the high ruined wall of a mid-thirteenth-century Norman castle stands beside the bridge. This was a frontier in the Middle Ages and the crossing was defended against those who would raid down from the plateau.

Over the bridge, when after a few kilometres the road climbs zig-zagging up the escarpment face, the outer defences come into view. At a pass, a mere notch in the edge of the plateau, there stands a flat-topped earthen mound, or 'motte'. This, built at the behest of an invading Norman baron, was once crowned by a wooden palisade and a timber blockhouse, guarding the river plain against the mountain. Beyond it the land is poor, the view somewhat dreary, the signs of habitation relatively few. It is a land of stubborn survival, while the river valley below is a corridor of change.

This particular discontinuity, occasioned by a rise in elevation of hardly a hundred metres, marks a long and complicated geological history. The high ground consists of shales and coal-measures, rocks of the Upper Carboniferous, which had long been buried under later formations and then, in the long ages of geological time, had been exposed again as these bleak uplands. Only in one or two other stretches of the country do these formations occur — in west Kerry and west Clare at the Shannon mouth, and in the border regions of south-west Ulster — but where they do, a similar contrast in landscapes will be found along their borders. And a similar historical significance. They provide one type of Braudel's 'mountains' and are areas of conservative survival.

But there are other types too. Into the comparatively small area of Ireland there fit the evidences of many episodes in the natural history of the earth. As islands go, of course, Ireland is comparatively large — twentieth in size on a scale which takes Australia as the largest island. But unlike most islands it has most of the higher ground at the periphery, not the centre. It has a largely lowland interior. Although the high ground is not in fact very high, Irish mountains give the impression of being much greater than they actually are. The light plays tricks in the moisture-laden air.

This light changes from minute to minute, and works its own visual deceptions. The near appears far and the far appears near. It gives a distinctive quality to the view of Ireland. It makes manifest the presence of the surrounding ocean, source of the clouds that drift on the ever-changing skies and of the rain that gives the country its famous greenness. Nowhere in the country is more than eighty kilometres from the sea.

Because of the highland rim to the island, most of the Irish rivers of any size flow inland before making their way to the sea. There are many hundreds of large and small lake. There are great expanses of bog, spanned by vast skies and characterised by their lonely beauty. There is a myriad of slow winding streams.

Part of Ireland's scenic variety derives from the fact that within the country two of the main structural landforms of western Europe intersect — the Caledonian mountain ranges striking southwest from Norway through Scotland into Ulster in the north and Connacht in the west of Ireland, and the Armorican folds running west from central Germany through western France and southern Britain to form a series of parallel ranges in Munster in the south of Ireland. These ranges run out into the Atlantic with drowned valleys between them in the finger-like peninsulas of Cork and Kerry which are separated by fjord-like bays.

In the angle formed by this major intersection of rock-structures lie Ireland's central lowlands. Most of this well-watered interior is limestone, usually with a covering of drift, or 'boulder clay' deposited as sediments from the great thickness of ice which covered most of the land little more than ten thousand years ago. That drift in turn, and in time, produced a growth of forest, of grasslands, and of spreading bogs. Century after century the people who inhabited the island cleared the trees, until there was virtually no virgin forest left. With rare exceptions, the Irish woods of today derive from plantations of comparatively recent times.

Apart from the main structures, there are many other landforms, such as the volcanic and metamorphous rocks which form mountain ranges in Antrim, Down and Wicklow. These produce abrupt local changes in the landscape, often more dramatic than that to be observed in the Barrow valley at Carlow. These changes not only document the episodes of an eventful geological history but show to the discerning eye the framework of the human history that came afterwards.

The contrasts have been blurred somewhat by the action of the last great modifying influence of Ireland's geology, the ice. We speak of the 'Ice Age' as of something in the distant past. In fact we live in it. It is a period of fluctuating climate in which episodes of intense cold are separated by warm 'inter-glacial' episodes. There have been four major phases of great cold and three long warm intervals. We are now at the beginning of the fourth 'interglacial'. The last period of severe cold ended about ten thousand years ago, when the regions of permanent snow and ice extended far from the poles, locking up in frozen form a great deal of the earth's water and so lowering sea-levels.

Ireland lies in quite northerly latitudes (between 51° and 56°, the latitude of Labrador or northern Kamchatka) and was severely affected by the glaciation. In the most recent cold phase a great thickness of ice extended southward over most of the country, while a separate local system of glaciers blanketed the south-west. The action of the ice, as the glaciers shifted, melted, re-froze, or flowed inch by inch with their content of sediments and frozen-in rocks, ground down the jagged profiles of mountains, scooped out valleys, spread deposits of clay and mud, and generally softened and blurred the contours of the land. The mark of this activity (which happened only yesterday, in geological terms) is everywhere to be seen in Ireland.

It blurs, without erasing, the local contrasts. There is, throughout the country, a feeling of local intimacy that arises from every corner of the island being subtly different from every other. This affects the people. The sense of local particularism is very strong. A popular song celebrates Ireland's 'forty shades of green'. The people too come in forty shades (of green and orange, it might be said, among other hues). Each county of the thirty-two that make up the whole of Ireland, each parish, is believed to have its own characteristics.

The most striking broad contrasts at the present day are probably those between east and west. This is largely due to differences in climate and land. A line ruled on a map of Ireland from south-west to north-east will crudely separate two contrasting zones. The west is wetter and has the most extensive areas of mountain, bog and poor land. It is here that old ways and beliefs have most stubbornly survived. The somewhat higher rainfall is probably the most important factor. Even in periods of optimum climate in historical times (such as the thirteenth century) the ruled line roughly marks the feasible limit of wheat cultivation, for example. The land to the west was difficult to cultivate, difficult to colonise and settle. Many extensive tracts to the present day are virtually uninhabitable. In some areas, such as parts of west Mayo, the traces can still be seen of desperate attempts to cultivate barren hillsides a century and a half ago, when whole populations lived on the potato before the failure of that crop led to the great famine of the 1840s.

The west, with its mountains, great bays, bogs and salmon-streams, is the part of Ireland attractive to tourists but with the smallest number of permanent inhabitants. The better lands of the east have attracted visitors of a different sort — invaders, settlers, conquerors — down the ages. The land has been tamed by Irish, Norse, Norman, Scottish and English farmers, and has been transformed by traders, administrators, reformers, builders, planners, entrepreneurs and proletarian settlers. In recent decades the east-west contrast has become more marked, as there was a considerable east-west population shift.

Ireland is now an urbanised country, with about three quarters of its population living in towns or cities. This is most noticeable in the east. The numbers in the total population were in continuous decline for more than a century after the fearful famine of the 1840s, but have been increasing since the 1960s. The increase may just now (in 1985) have been checked. By 1980 the figure approached five million people, about as many as inhabited Ireland in 1800 (there were more than eight million by 1841, just before the Famine). But the distribution today is quite different. In

1800 there was only one large city, Dublin, which was then about a fifth of its present size. There was a dense and rapidly growing rural population. Everywhere in the countryside people were in evidence, and the cabins and shacks in which they subsisted. And the countryside then, outside the estate walls, was bare, stripped of timber.

Now, a quarter of the total population lives in or near Dublin, and rather more than half as many live in or near Belfast, a city which in 1800 had only twenty thousand people. The towns all sprawl out into the countryside through newly built housing estates, detached bungalows, small factories, new school buildings, and new churches.

The traveller in Ireland will soon notice other contrasts, besides those that the bones of the landscape provide. There are areas that are tidy, trim, well tilled. There are areas that are neglected, slovenly, where weeds grow in the fields. This is nowhere a simple country: its cultural patterns are as complicated by local variation as its history. One obvious contrast derives from the existence for the past sixty years of two political systems in the island. This too has by now left its mark on the landscape. The road system in Northern Ireland, for example, is better and better maintained than that of the Republic, although, bearing in mind the much higher density of population there, it is comparatively little used. The empty motorways of the North show the operation of a system whose basis is not local. They serve as a reminder of the influence which can't long be avoided in any discussion of Ireland, that of the larger neighbouring island of Great Britain.

This influence indeed will be immediately obvious to the outside observer with an eye, say, for architecture, or for the lay-out of an estate. It provides one of the most interesting visual elements in the country. Ireland doesn't look English (and the English visitor will find it in many ways foreign) but it certainly looks, not surprisingly, as if the English spent a long time there. The domestic architecture in particular, while having its own peculiarities, is closer to English work than to any Continental style. It is, in fact, what we can recognise as a colonial style.

Landscape leads to history. The rocks, the shapes of the mountains, the configuration of the lakes, reveal their own story, their natural history of the shaping of the land by the forces of nature. But superimposed on them is the abundant evidence of ten thousand years of human activity. While much of the Irish landscape is still untamed, everywhere people have made their own marks on it. The visitor coming in to land at Shannon from over the Atlantic, will descend over a landscape of rocks and lakes that in some aspects looks as primeval and untamed as Labrador. But a second glance shows that it has been intricately colonised and worked over, with little fields, ancient earthworks, castles, ruined churches, roads, farms, villages, utilising whatever of nature could be tamed. People have been here for a long time.

2

PEOPLES AND SETTLEMENT

In the recurrent warm intervals of the Ice Age human hunting groups entered lowland Britain, but so far we have no certain evidence of any inhabitation of Ireland during this immensely long period. During the last general glaciation dry land extended far to the south of Ireland's present southern shores, and it is more than likely that there were people there. But it is not certain.

After the withdrawal of the ice, forests gradually spread northwards through Europe. People adapted to the changed conditions, and some groups already accustomed to forest conditions probably drifted northwards. The Ice Age hunters had preyed on large mammals, such as mammoth or reindeer, in fairly open tundra-like conditions. Now people lived increasingly on somewhat smaller game — red deer, roe deer, birds, fish — and on an increasing abundance of vegetable food, including nuts, berries, edible seeds and fungi in season. Their cultures are termed 'Mesolithic' (Middle Stone Age). Mesolithic people lived in Ireland soon after the ice withdrawal, having no doubt arrived as part of this general movement and adaptation. Both Ireland and Britain were still connected by land to the Continent before the rising sea-level made of them the islands they are today.

The archaeological remains of the Mesolithic people in Ireland provide a meagre record. But it gives some information. They derived at least some of their food supply from what was available on the shores of sea, lake and stream — and it would seem that there was an abundance. We may envisage small bands, in the centuries after the withdrawal of the ice, following the shores and waterways into the Irish interior and adjusting, generation after generation, to the local conditions. Early hunting populations were small, but the Irish environment as the climate improved would have provided sustenance for increasing numbers. It is not only possible but likely that the people living among the forests began to exercise some direct control over their food supply, as distinct from simply waiting for nature to supply them. This 'pre-adaptation', the first stage in the long process of transition to food production, is widespread and has been observed in many parts of the world.

The Mesolithic population probably rose in course of time from a few thousand to some tens of thousands. The numbers may seem very small in comparison with modern populations, but in all probability those hunters and gatherers, now so distant from us in time, formed the basic genetic stock of 'the Irish people'. It is also probable that the origins of the first immigrant mesolithic bands were diverse. New, small, groups of people would have arrived from time to time, from different places, with new ideas, languages and equipment. For a long time there was room for all.

Some time, perhaps about five thousand years BC, full Neolithic economies began to be established here and there. The cultures of the 'new stone age' were already ancient by then in parts of Europe, and voyagers to Ireland (which was now an island) must have introduced at least some of their features. Domesticated plants and animals, not indigenous in the island, were brought in. Some of the Mesolithic groups, without abandoning all their old ways, appear to have acquired the new techniques, along with animals and seeds. Pastoralism and tillage begin, and we have evidence from several parts of the country of neolithic villages, where the people kept cattle and sowed grain crops.

The new ideas appear to have reached Ireland both from the Atlantic, or western, Neolithic cultures which had spread by sea along the western coasts of Europe, and from the main Central European cultures which had spread slowly overland to reach Britain from the east and south. As these ideas were absorbed by the Mesolithic people, or their descendants, a mixed economy developed, and a variety of cultural traditions throughout the island. The techniques of forest clearance used by Neolithic farmers — by 'slash-and-burn', for example — had unexpected and unintended effects. Some types of bog spread rapidly, especially over early tillage areas whose available soil had been rapidly exhausted. The disturbance to the natural vegetation was considerable.

But the population rose, perhaps, by the end of the long Neolithic period, to one or two hundred thousand. The cultivators used wooden and stone hoes on small plots, or gardens. It is possible that here as elsewhere the initiators of this great economic revolution were women. Only a shallow light soil was suitable for their methods. When they sought grazing lands too, the Neolithic herders sought light soils which did not support a heavy forest growth — mainly drift-free soils on high ground above the densely wooded valleys. But the Neolithic people had implements well suited to the working of wood, including the polished stone axes (a very efficient woodsman's tool) which are found on their settlements everywhere in Europe. Some of them built long rectangular houses of wooden post construction, supporting rafters and thatch, broadly in a wide-spread European tradition. Variants of this house-type continued into modern times in rural Ireland.

It is probable, to judge by the more abundant evidence from comparable communities in Europe, that the earlier Neolithic people lived

The Shannon at Clonmacnoise, Co. Offaly

Skellig Monastery, Co. Kerry

The Giant's Causeway, Co. Antrim

Dún Anghusa, on the Cliffs of Inishmore, Aran Islands

The Bourne Vincent Memorial Park, Killarney, Co. Kerry

Clew Bay, Westport, Co. Mayo

with little social differentiation, in villages of more or less equal peasant families. But as time went by things must have changed. The later Neolithic people have left great and imposing monuments which imply both complexity and hierarchy in social organisation.

There are two groups, or families, of megalithic chambered tombs built in neolithic times in Ireland. In one group, a round mound was heaped over an inner tomb structure of very large stones. In the other group the mound was long, often rectangular. The two groups are contemporary, or at least overlap in time, but the difference in tomb-shape reflects other differences in the style of objects and materials buried with the dead, while at the same time there is much in common.

In the largest form the long barrows (or mounds) — up to 60 metres overall — have open courts, or fore-courts, from which covered galleries built of massive stones may be entered. This type is very numerous in a fairly dense band running across Ireland from Killala and Donegal bays to Carlingford Lough and, beyond the Channel, to the Firth of Clyde. Many other examples survive in the northern half of Ireland, but south of the line Dublin-Galway there are only two or three. Smaller tombs, apparently connected with this type, are more widespread. These are usually seen denuded of their mounds so that they exhibit what is often the stark grandeur of the megalithic structure. They are nowadays known as 'portal graves' or 'portal dolmens'. For many centuries they have impressed people as the work of giants; there is a description of a 'giant's grave' in a text as early as the seventh century.

The round mounds are interestingly different. Their builders often arranged them in hilltop cemeteries, in each of which there are usually mounds of widely varying size clustered closely together. Some are huge, a single mound covering half a hectare. The mound has a surrounding kerb of massive stones, set on edge and end to end. It covers a passage, formed of great standing-stones, close-set and spanned by lintel-stones, which leads into a burial chamber, also formed of great stones and sometimes roofed by a false dome (a corbelled vault). There are usually smaller chambers leading off the main vault.

Passage-grave cemeteries have a scattered distribution, but the greater number again is in the northern half of the island. The most remarkable cemetery by far is that whose focus is along a short stretch of the river Boyne, about 20 Km upstream from the river mouth. Here among many smaller tombs, are three huge mounds, two of which, at Newgrange and Knowth, have been partly excavated. They are remarkable in scale and size and in the basic, but far from trivial, engineering skills that went into their construction. Some of them, especially in the Boyne group, are also most elaborately carved with mysterious abstract-seeming symbols — spirals, concentric circles, meanders, zig-zags, lozenges, branching linear forms and other devices.

The evidence for the burial ritual also reveals elaboration. They are collective tombs, in which deposits of clean washed cremated bone (of many individuals) were made. It seems that the bodies of the dead were first placed in temporary burials or mortuary houses to decay. Construction of the tombs was carefully and accurately planned, with due regard to orientation. In the tomb of Newgrange the sun, just after it rises at midwinter, shines through a specially made aperture just over the entrance and along the 20-m. passage to illuminate the stone at the rear of the end chamber.

The tombs imply a system of religious belief and much more. There must have been experts of various kinds — priests, engineers, gangers, carvers. The monuments, older than the Great Pyramid, raise many questions.

About 2000 BC it appears that people were beginning to exploit metallic ores (especially copper) in Ireland. Metal industries had long been established by then in south-western and south-eastern Europe. As populations expanded, as tribal migrations on a large scale began, these industries introduced the dynamic of long-distance trade and communications to the comparatively static world of isolated Neolithic communities. Ireland was fairly rich in copper ores, and the metal prospectors began using these. Production and trade of flat axes and other metal objects began. Other cultural changes occurred about this time too, marked by changes in pottery styles and other such indexes employed by the archaeologists. There is evidence for the arrival in the country of further groups or bands (mainly it would seem of pastoralists) from the Continent.

There is a suggestion of more mobility, associated with both pastoralism and trade, but the evidence for settlement through much of what is conventionally termed the 'Bronze Age' is sparse. At least some groups in the country through this long period of fifteen hundred years or so displayed great skill in the production of metal objects, especially gold ornaments. Gold was apparently panned from some of the rivers, and formed the basis of an export industry at times. By about 1200 BC, when we can dimly discern further changes in Ireland, it is clear that there were pockets of quite considerable wealth. We may guess that chiefdoms of some kind had been established.

Another period of rapid and important change is observable about the seventh century BC. By then, peoples who spoke languages of Indo-European origin had imposed themselves almost all over Europe. In Central and western Europe the dominant chieftains belonged to one of the western branches of the Indo-Europeans — the Celts. Celtic-speaking people were well established by this date in England and France, and some

Celtic-speakers were probably settled, or settling, in Ireland. Improvements in agricultural methods may have contributed to a brief increase in prosperity about this time; but soon there was a climatic deterioration, and this may be associated with what appears to have been a general social retrogression lasting for some centuries.

Hilltop enclosures were occupied or used by tribal groups, or their chieftains, throughout most of the last millennium BC. Sometimes these are defensive in character, with ramparts and external ditches forming the enclosure; sometimes they seem to carry on the Early Bronze Age tradition of the sacred or ritual enclosure within which some sort of ceremonial was conducted. Much of the little settlement evidence we have for the last five hundred years or so BC comes from crannogs — artificial islands formed by laying layers of brushwood and stones in the shallows of lakes. Well-to-do families lived in them. An increasing uniformity of culture throughout the island is suggested by the evidence, brought about perhaps through the agency of some kind of specialised bardic class. But the climate continued to worsen. The rising waters of the lakes overwhelmed the Bronze-Age crannogs. Forest regressed on previously cultivated lands. We may guess at a falling population and a period of comparative isolation. There was a Dark Age of a kind, lasting for four or five centuries to about AD 200. But within this dark period important developments took place. The technology of iron was established in the country. The Romans conquered Celtic Gaul and then, in the first century AD, occupied Britain. They never came to Ireland.

By this time, written records are reasonably abundant in parts of Europe, and there are occasional references to Ireland, which so begins to emerge into history. The earliest accounts that give us some information on topography show that a Celtic language was spoken widely, at least by the first century AD. It is possible even to recognise some of the names that occur in the earliest literature in Irish some hundreds of years later. Irish is a language of the Celtic group and it had clearly been well established in the country by the time of Christ.

The Irish enter more forcefully into history with the decline of the Roman Empire in the west. By the fourth century we find them engaged in large-scale raids on Roman Britain, sometimes in alliance with the Picts (who lived beyond the frontier in what is now Scotland) and the Saxons from the distant shores of the North Sea beyond the imperial frontiers in Germany and Denmark. As the Roman power crumbled, Irish bands began colonising Britain, most successfully in Scotland, where the Gaelic language of Ireland was introduced when the Antrim kingdom of Dál Riada established a colony in Argyll.

By this stage we are beginning to acquire much more extensive information about the country. Written documents, at first very rare and sporadic, begin to be quite numerous. With their help we can just about discern — although still very dimly — the shaping of a new order in Ireland. Old tribal federations, or 'nations', were breaking up and being replaced by new dynastic groupings which were to dominate the scene for more than half a millennium.

Until the end of the eighth century there is no evidence for any further substantial immigration — although there are indications of some influx of refugees from the disturbed conditions of Gaul and elsewhere with the breakdown of the Roman empire in the West, as well as much coming and going of Christian churchmen — but Irish expansiveness opened up the country to all kinds of influences from outside. A vigorous development of culture ensued: the so-called 'Golden Age', with its high point in the eighth century.

This is an immensely rewarding period to study. Ireland became literate and Christian, and developed a distinctive civilization, without either passing through a phase of Roman occupation or being affected by the invasions and upheavals associated with the aftermath of the *Völkerwanderung* — the 'migration of peoples'. The British Celts underwent both these experiences, first being Romanized and then scattered and displaced by incoming Germans (the Anglo-Saxons). Some of the fragments of the ancient British society disappeared; others survived in peripheral areas, or by migration, as when a large group from the south settled part of western France and created *Bretagne*, Brittany, the country of the Britons.

The Irish, on the contrary, held their land and became intimately and indissolubly associated in their own minds with a clearly defined ancestral and, as it were, god-given (or goddess-given) territory: the island of Ireland. That powerfully felt association operates to the present day in Irish minds.

Ireland was feminine. The several names of the island are the names of goddesses, who are all manifestations of the same goddess. In the mythological history of the early Irish she is taken, ravished, by successive waves of male invaders. But the very first invasion is led by a woman, who is no doubt the primal goddess herself establishing her identity with the land. And thereafter, the lovers of the goddess of place, or sovereignty, the kings, are little more than her playthings. They are, each, a consort for a night (which is how the length of their reign is symbolized) to be replaced next evening by another lover. So Ireland is manifest in the earliest texts, and it is one of the distinctive oddities of the country that so Ireland is quite frequently represented to the present day.

3

MYTH AND LEGEND

Language is one of the major shaping elements of culture. For two thousand years or more the great majority of the people in Ireland spoke Irish as their native language. This indeed is the only language we know which itself was shaped in Ireland. It derived mainly from some form of Celtic, but also, to some degree, drew on words and forms from the languages spoken by prehistoric inhabitants of the island. For want of written records of those early times, however, we have no further information on the prehistoric languages.

Irish survives, barely, as a living tongue. Modern dialects of it are spoken still in parts of Donegal, Mayo, Galway, Kerry, Cork and Waterford. The closely related dialects of Scottish Gaelic are spoken by somewhat more numerous communities in the Scottish Highlands and Isles. Native speakers of all these dialects put together now number considerably less than 100,000 in total. The area of spoken Irish, or Gaelic, has been diminishing now for half a millennium. But in Tudor times Irish could fairly be described as the most widespread language of the British Isles, being spoken through most of Ireland, a large part of Scotland and the Isle of Man. The written, or scholarly, form of the language was standardized over this culture-area, and there was a vigorous living literature as well as a great body of older writings, going back as far as the sixth century A.D.

This literature includes prose and verse materials of all kinds. Its earliest texts embody much lore that was transmitted orally for many generations before the beginning of writing, so that it gives us unique glimpses of the world of pre-Roman western Europe. It provides, as the Celtic scholar Kenneth Jackson put it, 'a window on the Iron Age'. Indeed, if we peer hard through the window, we can see, however dimly, far beyond the Iron Age, for the legends and myths appear to include a great deal that is pre-Celtic. And if we look forward towards the present day we find a wealth of folklore and folk-custom in Ireland, some of which has a continuous connection with the almost unimagineably remote Neolithic age. That the Romans never arrived in Ireland allowed an ancient and free European spirit to carry through from the distant past its peculiar temperament and outlook without serious interruption.

The continuity makes connection not only with a remote past but also, to some extent, with places outside Ireland, especially those where Celtic-derived languages survived into the historic period. Welsh literature is nearly as old as Irish literature and there are many striking parallels between the two. Since about the middle of the last century Celtic scholars have taken as their province all the languages and literatures of the peoples whose histories go back to the Celtic-speaking cultures of late prehistoric Europe. They have illuminated the connections that reflect common institutions and traditions. A fine synthesis by Alwyn and Brinley Rees, for example, first published in 1961, under the title *Celtic Heritage*, takes as a basis the old stories of these literatures. It tries to reconstruct something of the tradition 'of which the stories, even in their original form' were but one expression.

It is usual to refer to the tales which appear in early medieval Irish manuscripts under four headings — designating groups or cycles — and to speak of the Mythological Cycle, the Ulster Cycle, the Fenian Cycle and the Historical Cycle. The stories of the Mythological Cycle deal chiefly with the *Tuatha Dé Danann*, the 'peoples of the goddess Danu', who were said to have inhabited Ireland before the coming of the 'Milesians', ancestors of the Gaelic-speaking people. The Fenian Cycle concerns the adventures of Finn mac Cumhaill and his hunting and fighting bands (the *Fianna*): medieval romantic tales. The Ulster Cycle deals with the warriors of the Ulaid and in particular with the hero Cuchulainn: early sagas. The Historical Cycle, more diversified in its contents and personnel, treats of the shadowy period about the dawn of history and consists partly of saga-tales concerning dimly known historical figures.

They can be read, out of context, simply as wonder tales or entertainments, like the Arabian Nights entertainments or the fairy tales of a foreign land. But they were something more than mere entertainment to the people who composed them and to those who first enjoyed them, for they express their attitudes to life and the world and their ideas about history, geography, humankind and the universe.

Like any other form of literature they make numerous assumptions about the audience. A great deal is taken for granted as being common ground between those who told the stories and those to whom they were told.

It is assumed, for example, that the Irish audience will have a detailed knowledge of Irish places and place-names, and a knowledge of a particular kind. *'Dindshenchus'*, the lore of places, was part of the common culture. Almost every place which found a niche in the literature had a story or an attribute attached to it. This is interesting because it survives so vigorously in Ireland today, where popular ballads may consist of little more than strings of placenames, where the question, 'Where are you from?', is one of the first to be asked, and where there is an elaborate and minute lore about the particular characteristics attributable to various places or to the people who come from them.

The stories also assume a knowledge of the framework of the literature itself and of the pseudo-history of Ireland. All kinds of references are made which take it for granted that the audience is familiar with names and episodes, just as today a Christmas pantomime, ostensibly dealing with Red Riding Hood or Puss-in-Boots, will be full of references to current politics or to well-known shows on television. All this, of course, is lost when the stories are read out of context for entertainment or for scholarly reasons which are not directly concerned with their content.

It is however possible to reconstruct at least part of this general frame of reference, as the Rees brothers, among others, have done, and to tease out some of the major themes which can lead to a better understanding of the cosmogony and beliefs of the early peoples of Britain and Ireland.

The apprehension of time and space is a basic matter. For time, we have an early source which happens to have survived not in an insular context but in Continental Europe. The Coligny Calendar sets forth the Gaulish year — in fact a period of five years, which seems to have been of special significance to the Gauls. From the study of the calendar it would appear that the idea of the duality of light and dark was dominant. One of the peculiarities of Celtic calendar-custom on the Continent which was remarked on by the Romans was that they counted nights rather than days.

In fact the reckoning was more complex, but the dualism of day and night, winter and summer, light and dark, is very marked. So it is that moments in between the dualities are magical and dangerous. Sunrise and sunset were dangerous periods, and the great festivals occurred at the junctions of the year, when winter was passing into summer at May Eve, and when summer was passing into winter at November Eve. The supernatural breaks through at these dangerous moments, and there was a kind of chaos before the order of the universe was restored with the establishment of the new day and the new season.

In Ireland there were four major festivals, corresponding to such turning points: *Samhain* at the beginning of November, *Imbolc* at the beginning of February, *Beltaine* at the beginning of May, and *Lughnasa* at the beginning of August. Clusters of customs associated with these ancient festivals survived until recent times, although they were usually given a superficially Christian meaning. Sets of customs associated with one of them were analysed and discussed in a splendid book, *The Festival of Lughnasa*, by Máire MacNeill, a model and a classic of its kind. She examined in it the customs and traditions centering on 'Garland Sunday' at the end of July or the beginning of August. Elements of great antiquity emerged, in reminiscences of the widely known great Celtic god *Lug* (after whom a number of Continental places were known in Roman times as *Lug-dunum*, to give modern place-names such as Lyon, Loudun, Leiden and Laon), or the more local and Irish *Crom Dubh*. Many of the stories and customs relating to Lug were transferred to St. Patrick. People went on with their old cult, but gave it a Christian name. One of the most remarkable annual events in modern Ireland, the pilgrimage in late July which brings thousands of people to toil barefoot up the steep scree-strewn slopes of Croagh Patrick in County Mayo, is a survival of the *Lughnasa* festival, which was celebrated by assemblies on hilltops.

But there are other customs at that same time of year which seem to have a more recent origin, at least so far as Ireland is concerned. These include the famous Puck Fair at Killorglin in County Kerry, where a male goat is exalted for the three days of the event on a platform above the throng.

Apart from the major festivals there were many customs and observances marking the passage of the year, some very ancient, others introduced in recent times. Perhaps calendar customs are one of the best witnesses to the diversity of the sources of Irish tradition. Nowadays, most of them have died out, as modern communications have tended steadily towards uniformity of behaviour, between town and country, between one place and another. Some customs have been widely diffused as a result of this tendency to uniformity — Christmas trees and Santa Claus, for example, in quite recent times. A few, like the Hallowe'en customs, have been diffused outwards, and stubbornly survive; but by and large the changing seasons of the year have much less significance for the Irish today than they had for their ancestors. Gradually the old patterns associated with rural life or with the life of merchant towns have yielded to the patterns of life in industrialized society.

St. Brigid's Day, the first of February, replaced the old festival of *Imbolc* (marking, according to an ancient source, 'the beginning of the lactation of the ewes'). This was once observed in every part of Ireland and was taken to mark the beginning of spring. There was considerable variety of celebration. A common feature was the traditional 'St. Brigid's cross', made in a remarkable variety of local forms, which was nailed above the byre or otherwise displayed to protect in particular the dairy and the farm animals. A stylized version of this emblem has been adopted as the symbol of RTE, the national broadcasting service of the Republic of Ireland.

What is striking is not the antiquity of some calendar customs but the extent to which the various immigrations are represented in them. The wearing of harvest knots in Armagh or Cork, the performances of mummers in Dublin or Wexford, sporadic survivals of traditional carol-singing, and many more items mark the arrival of settlers from outside

Ireland in the centuries since the Anglo-Norman advent in the twelfth century, and represent overlays of tradition on the old Gaelic pattern. The Irish tradition of the eighteenth and nineteenth centuries was one to the making of which many strands had gone.

One of the most interesting calendar customs, still strongly maintained, is the celebration of the anniversary of the battle of the Boyne (which happened in 1690) on the twelfth of July each year. It seems that some of the associated customs, such as the Belfast one of lighting bonfires, may be imitative, counter-demonstrations to the midsummer bonfires of Catholics. The Twelfth is the great Ulster Protestant day of celebration, marked chiefly by the custom of marching with banners and drums. But this custom was once widespread and was by no means confined to the Orange party. We may have in the festival of the Boyne, as in many others, a synthesis formed in the past few centuries, largely with borrowed elements.

The characters in the early Irish sagas are not historical. Some, at best, are 'pseudo-historical' (using the names of people who may actually have lived, but fitting them into elaborate fictions). They include gods and goddesses and there are many mythological overtones. Like epic in other literatures — Greek, Sanskrit, Norse, and so on — they relate to a prehistoric period, somewhat different from the time of the society that was entertained by listening to their recital. They belong to the class of early literatures described as 'heroic', literature dealing with figures larger than life, who lived in a simpler time, belonged to the aristocratic class of a society which subsisted largely on the plunder of cattle or other valuables from neighbouring areas, and practised the art and trade of war. Homer's *Iliad* depicts such a society.

Epic, the entertainment provided by bards who recited the doings of mighty deeds, to divert kings and nobles in royal halls with stories of fabulous ancestors, shows us a world that existed before writing began. In Irish literature this is particularly true of the Ulster Cycle. The cycle is a group of sagas dealing with the warrior society of the ancient kingdom of the Ulaid, whose royal centre was at *Emhain Mhacha* (Navan fort, beside Armagh) and whose king was Conchobhar mac Nesa.

It is a simple society that is shown, and only part of it is depicted in the literature. The storytellers themselves, in later times at least, placed the reign of Conchobhar mac Nesa about the time of Christ. In fact the world depicted in *Táin Bó Cuailgne* and other narratives of the cycle, is probably that of a somewhat later time. But much of the description would fit an earlier period, not in Ireland, but in Continental Europe.

One of the many indications we have that the society depicted in the *Táin* and others of the Ulster tales is not wholly imaginary but has some basis in reality is that it closely matches what Greek and Latin writers tell us about the way of life of the Celts of Continental Europe some centuries before the time of Christ. Some of the similarities are so striking, in spite of the time gap, that we must assume a common fund of traditions, institutions and ideas, some of which survived to a very late date in Ireland, long after they had disappeared elsewhere. At the head of this society was a king, leader of a group of warrior nobles whom he controlled and appeased through war and the distribution of booty. The lower orders of society don't figure in the sagas, since the storytellers and their clients had no interest in them.

But certain superior craftsmen do. Some of their crafts were associated with magical skills and mysteries which conferred relatively high status.

Certain classes dealt in one way or another with the otherworld of the supernatural. Druids were priests, prophets and magicians. They could read omens and foretell the future. They were teachers, and they imparted learning to their pupils by intoning information which was repeated back to them in chorus — a method of instruction by no means obsolete today. The Greek writer Strabo tells of three classes of learned men among the Gauls, the bards, the *vates* or prophets, and the druids. These are *bard, fáith* and *druí* in the Irish literature, one of the most striking correspondences. Besides these specialists, the king also was an intermediary, not only between his kingdom or tribe and its neighbours, whether friendly or hostile, in this world, but also between his tribe and the mysterious otherworld.

But the correspondences are numerous. 'When they dine', wrote Diodorus Siculus of the Gauls, 'they have hearths with big fires and cauldrons and spits loaded with big joints of meat. They honour distinguished men with the best portions of the meat . . . And when they are dining, some of the company often fall into an altercation and challenge one another to single combat — they make nothing of death. Whenever anyone will accept their challenges, they set about glorifying the valour of their forefathers and boasting of their own prowess; and at the same time they deride and belittle their opponents, and try by their speeches to rob him of all the courage he has in his heart.' All of this, with uncanny faithfulness, is to be found in the Irish sagas: this very custom, just as described, is the theme of *The Story of Mac Dá Thó's Pig*.

The early Irish had a pantheon, just as the Greeks and Romans had. It seems less orderly than theirs, largely because of the lack of a strictly contemporary literature to tidy it up — it comes to us through the censorious medium of Christian writings — but the general Indo-European pattern can be discerned. The pantheon reflects the male-dominated pastoral society which we know from our early historical records. In modern India the idea of the unity of God was largely left to intellectuals. Brahma existed, if at all, on so high a plane as to be beyond the vision of ordinary people, and even Visnu and Siva tended to be displaced, for their respective followers, by more homely manifestations, and the whole structure of the pantheon to rest, in practice, on humble, local, and often animistic cults. So it probably was in Ireland.

Marie-Louise Sjoestedt pointed out in her book on *Gods and Heroes of the Celts* that 'in the historical tradition . . . the principal role belongs to colonisers, inventors or male warriors, and female persons intervene only in episodes. On the other hand, in the "geographical" tales of the *Dindshenchus* the female divinities fill a much larger place. This is explained by what has already been observed from the Gaulish evidence, namely, the national or tribal character of the gods and the local character of the goddesses'.

This, of course, is not unusual. It illustrates the way in which religions, in practice as distinct from theory, exist simultaneously on different levels and often accommodate apparently discarded systems of belief within an enlarged framework. Anu, Danu and Brigit, the principal goddesses whose names survive, had a variety of local manifestations, and probably often merely presided in name over ancient nature-worshipping cults. They may have become involved with — or may derive from — goddesses from the pre-Celtic prehistoric past. The continued sacred character into the beginning of historic times of the old Neolithic and Bronze Age burial sites would suggest this.

But it is the male figures who dominate the recorded tradition — the Dagda, Nuadu, Lug and others. The Dagda is a figure of primitive force, wielding a magic club, excessive in his appetites. Lug is of a different character, usually represented as young and beautiful. They move about in the real world, and Ireland was full of places associated with the gods. Part of the force of the old storytelling comes from the presence of the otherworld, not in some remote place, but invisibly in, about and around this world. The interaction of the two worlds was the most powerful in those ambiguous situations, which the storytellers were fond of imagining, between light and dark, neither inside nor outside a house, neither on nor off the ground.

There is a theme which recurs. It is not unknown in other traditions but in the Irish literature it is applied in a particular way. It represents beauty embracing ugliness. It is like the theme of the princess and the frog in the German fairy-tale, except that in the Irish versions ugliness does not take the form of a prince, but of a queen. Or rather, of sovereignty; for that is the meaning in the earliest recensions.

The theme is exemplified in the story of Niall of the Nine Hostages, in his youth. His brothers rejected the advances of a hideous old hag whom they met on the way, but he lay with her, whereupon she was revealed as a beautiful woman, who announced to him that she was Sovereignty and that by possessing her he possessed kingship. So he came to rule at Tara. The idea of wedding the sovereignty was apparently embodied in ceremonies connected with early Irish kingship. The ceremony known as the *féis* of Tara, for example, as James Carney and others have pointed out, probably included a symbolic or enacted mating of some kind. And the sovereignty goddess (Medb of Tara is an example) when she figures in stories, is often represented as a woman who takes many lovers, who serve her. A variation is suggested in an account given by Gerald of Wales at the end of the twelfth century of the inauguration ceremony of a local king in the north who apparently coupled with a mare and then drank broth made from her flesh. His successors, incidentally, were inaugurated in medieval times on an eminence called Doon Rock, in County Donegal, near which is Doon Well, the scene to the present day of customs almost as strange.

The personification of sovereignty becomes in the tradition something slightly different: the personification of the kingdom. In time the woman whose beauty is revealed to the rightful sovereign becomes Ireland — a powerful myth which survived through medieval literature into modern times. In Jacobite verse of the eighteenth century the beauty is no longer hidden by ugliness, as a rule, but is seen by the poet in a dream or vision. The woman shows her beauty (which is elaborately described) but laments because she is married to the wrong spouse, the false (Hanoverian) sovereign. Her rights will be restored only when the true (Stuart) king returns from over the water. Sometimes, in the later verse, Ireland (or perhaps the sovereignty) appears in other guise, although still displaying beauty or value — as a brown cow, for example, the finest of the kine, when one myth borrows reinforcement from another.

These images passed into modern romanticism and sentimentality about Ireland. The harsh quality of the early versions, where the young hero, to win kingship, was required to mate with a hag of hideous aspect and unpleasant demeanour, was softened. The hag, insofar as she survived in the tradition, was sentimentalized into the Shan Van Vocht (*seanbhean bhocht* — poor old woman), everybody's poor old granny. The 'Caesar', or hero, coming over the sea, lost some of his quality too —

The French are on the say
Says the Shan Van Vocht.

Or Ireland became the weeping beauty with the stringless harp, a wolfhound at her feet, a Round Tower behind her, silhouetted against a sunburst in the imagery of the new nationalism which dispensed with the 'rightful king'.

Yet, softened and sentimentalized although it was, the image still had potency. It occurs still in one of the favourite songs of Ulster nationalists, 'The Four Green Fields'. It was this sentimentalized image that the innovating Taoiseach, Sean Lemass, singled out, towards the end of his career, as one to be abandoned. He wanted Ireland to become a modestly prosperous bourgeois republic, and he sensed that the Poor Old Woman, whom he called on the country to forget, not merely concealed the beauty of the being whose true name is Sovereignty, but has long been the Irish version of the death goddess.

Like other symbols and images of the period of romantic nationalism, that of Ireland personified has faded very much in the Republic, where independence gradually brought about concern with everyday and mundane affairs and a diminishing response to the old stimuli of patriotic fervour. It has been otherwise in the North, where, among the nationalist part of the population, sentimental and romantic imagery still has the power to move. The poor old woman, lamenting the loss of her fourth green field (the partioned province, Ulster) shows her white-haired, sentimental, aspect there. She seems long removed from the hideous hag whom early kings embraced. But that hag presumably had a good Indo-European ancestry, and her description in the early stories matches well that of another, at the farther end of the Indo-European world, Kali, or Durga, with her necklace of skulls, her lolling red tongue, her carnivorous tusks, and her many arms bearing weapons. Kali, the wife of Siva the Destroyer, dances in the North, and she has not yet resumed her benevolent aspect as Sati the Virtuous, or Parvati.

The meanings of old myths have been pressed unduly into the service of politics. Although the old image of Sovereignty as a woman had, on the face of it, to do with political situation, its meaning was not really concerned with them. It referred rather to the good ordering of the universe.

Kingship, in the early concept, belonged as much to the order of nature as to that of politics. The rightful king was to be recognized and discerned by signs which showed that he was the one chosen and fitted by the gods to act as intermediary between the powers of nature and the world of men and women. This concept, although diluted, persisted right down to the eighteenth-century Jacobite poems. The exile over the water whose return the poems anticipated was still 'the one who is born to be king' — born, not elected. It is only at the point of change when the French fleet is awaited to carry, not the pre-ordained king but the rationalism of a republic that confusion begins. But, even yet, it persists, with the hope that the poor old woman will suddenly be seen to be, as in Yeats's play: *a young girl, and she had the walk of a queen.*

Other goddesses have survived in strange ways. A thousand years ago, the Irish had, on the first of February, one of the principal celebrations of their ecclesiastical year. As we have seen, five hundred years earlier this was the festival of *Imbolc* before it became St. Brigid's Day.

The early references to Imbolc indicate that it was an occasion which had to do with the calendar of a pastoral people, being connected with the fertility and renewal of flocks and herds. There is much stress on the topic of milk. For all this there are parallels elsewhere. The ancient Roman festival of *Lupercalia*, also in February, appears originally to have been a holiday of shepherds, in honour of the fertility god Lupercus, who was said to keep the wolves from the sheep.

Brigid herself, the patroness of the first of February, was, with Patrick and Columba, one of the three principal saints of the Irish. She differs from the other two, however, in an important respect. Both Patrick and Columba are figures of history. Under an accumulation of legend and folklore we can discern, for each of them, some historical reality, with a location in place and time. Some of Patrick's own writings survive, and for Columba we have the *Life* written by his successor in the abbacy of Iona, Adomnan, about a century after the saint's death. While this work is full of conventional hagiographical wonder-working, and while it undoubtedly contains much legendary material, there can be no doubt that Columba himself did live and work and have his place in the affairs of sixth-century Ireland and Scotland.

The oldest surviving *Life* of an Irish saint is the work on St. Brigid written by Cogitosus of Kildare, and it, too, like the work of Adomnan on Columba, was written about a century after the supposed date of the death of its subject. But in other ways the two *Lives* are quite different. Cogitosus gives us little more than a list of miracles concerned with butter-making and the like, together with some interesting information on the monastic city of Kildare in his own time, which was probably the middle of the seventh century. There are several other *Lives* of Brigid, quite early in date, but offering us no more real information about a tangible historical personage. They include a very early work in the Irish language (the other hagiography being in Latin).

This is not altogether surprising, for Brigid not only inherits the attributes but bears the name of one of the chief deities of the pagan Irish, the triple goddess who was also, it would seem, honoured by the Continental Celts of late prehistoric Europe. An early text, Cormac's Glossary, gives us some basic information:

> Brigit, that is a learned woman, daughter of the Dagda. That is Brigit woman of learning, that is a goddess whom poets worshipped. For her protecting care was very great and very wonderful. So they call her goddess of poets. Her sisters were Brigit woman of healing and Brigit woman of smith-work, daughters of the Dagda, from whose names among all the Irish a goddess was called Brigit.

This Brigit or Brigid appears to have belonged to the class of mother goddesses, whose equivalent is known from altars and inscriptions in Roman Gaul (the Matrones). According to the scholar T. F. O'Rahilly, her name derives from a form like *Briganti*, meaning something like 'the high goddess', which has derivatives also outside Ireland, as in the tribal names Brigantes, Brigantii. Brigantion, a tribal capital of the Brigantii, survives still in the name of the western Austrian town of Bregenz, on Lake Constance. In Ireland the goddess watched over childbirth, brought prosperity, and patronized poets and healers. A fowl was buried alive at the confluence of three streams in sacrifice to her, clearly marking her triple character.

Brigid the Christian saint, if she lacks historicity, inherited a great deal of the qualities of the goddess. Milk and butter, flocks and herds, figure largely in her *Lives*. She was born neither within nor without a house, but on the threshold, between night and day, and was washed in milk. According to the Old Irish *Life* she was reared on the milk of a white red-eared cow (this is how Otherworld cows appear in the stories), which saved her life when she was failing to survive on other sustenance. One of her miracles was to change water into milk (she could also, on occasion, turn it into ale). Another, occurring in several versions and variations, concerns the increase of flocks, or the marvellous replacement of beasts lost or stolen from a herd.

The scene of the life and miracles is mainly set in the south midlands; the time, the fifth or sixth century. Croghan Hill, in Offaly, plays a central part in the legends, as does Ardagh, Co. Longford, and its bishop St. Mel. But the place most closely associated with St. Brigid was her 'city', later known as Cell Dara, or Kildare. Gerald of Wales, the chronicler of the Norman incursion, visited Kildare in the late twelfth century, and describes the fire which was kept perpetually burning there.

Although in the time of Brigid there were twenty servants of the Lord here, Brigid herself being the twentieth, only nineteen have ever been here since her death until now, and the number has never increased. They all, however, take their turns, one each night, in guarding the fire. When the twentieth night comes, the nineteenth nun puts the log beside the fire and says: 'Brigid, guard your fire. This is your night.' And in this way the fire is left there, and in the morning, as usual, has been burnt and the fire is still burning.

The fire is surrounded by a hedge which is circular and made of withies, and which no male may cross . . . Moreover, because of a curse of the saint, goats never have young here.

He goes on to describe what is probably the Curragh of Kildare:

There are very fine plains hereabouts, which are called 'Brigid's pastures', but no one has dared to put a plough into them. It is regarded as miraculous that these pastures, even though all the animals of the whole province have eaten the grass down to the ground nevertheless when morning comes have just as much grass as ever.

Kildare may well have been, as R. A. S. Macalister and others have suggested, a pagan sanctuary before it became Christian. It was a dual monastic establishment, of monks and nuns in separate communities. In the seventh century, according to Cogitosus, the tomb-shrines of Brigid and her collaborator in the foundation, bishop Conlaed, stood by the altar of the divided church. However, it was the abbess who ruled.

According to the Old Irish *Life*, St. Mel said of Brigid: 'This virgin alone in Ireland shall have the episcopal ordination'. And the same work tells us that Brigid, and after her her succession of abbesses, always had a priest as charioteer to drive her about. Cogitosus claimed primacy over the churches of 'almost the whole island' for Kildare, but not long after he wrote it seems that the community of Armagh came to an agreement with Kildare by which priority, on terms, was allowed to the northern church.

Whatever the truth about the origins of Kildare and its mysterious founder, St. Brigid is surely a suitable patron for the Women's Liberation movement. If things had gone a little differently in the seventh century, the church in Ireland might (it is a fanciful thought) have come under the rule of a woman.

A vast amount of this lore was still in the living tradition a hundred years ago, and even in the early decades of the twentieth century when, after the establishment of the Irish Free State, the Folklore Collection began its intensive work of collection, the strands of transmission which connected the remotest prehistory with life in modern times were still unbroken.

Most of them have been broken by now, but quite a few old customs continue. Gods and saints, merged in a pattern of folklore, still preside over certain holy wells or other sacral places where people gather and make offerings on appointed festivals. At Doon Well in County Donegal, the offerings left by the devotees, some in the form of little mannikins, bring us startlingly back to the distant pagan past. At St. Brigid's Well near Liscannor in County Clare, the carefully tended shrines, with plaster statues which anachronistically depict Brigid as a great founding abbess of the high middle ages, are chock-a-block with holy pictures, rosaries and crutches and other props discarded and offered there in gratitude by the sick and the halt who had been cured by the virtue of the water. At St. Mullins in County Carlow, at Ardmore in County Waterford, and at a number of other such places annual throngs gather for the 'pattern' (patron's day) to proceed in the designated 'rounds' of prescribed 'stations', reciting traditional prayers, as once was done at hundreds of holy places around the island.

Once a year in late July great crowds of pilgrims toil up the slope of Croagh Patrick, which rises 2000 feet from the Atlantic shore of Clew Bay,

Tomb chamber with carved basin, Knowth, Co. Meath

A megalithic tomb at Carrowmore, Co. Sligo

Athgreany stone circle, Co. Wicklow

The Turoe Stone, Co. Galway

A manuscript page from the Book of Leinster, Trinity College, Dublin in honour of St. Patrick. In commemoration too, in a way, of the great god *Lug*. Lug, or *Lugh* survived in another branch of the folk-tradition as a hobgoblin — 'hop-o'-my-thumb Lugh' — *Lugh-chorpán* (literally 'Lugh-little-body'), whose offspring appears, appropriately enough, on St. Patrick's Day cards from Montreal to New Orleans, all in bright Kelly green: the leprechaun.

4
IRELAND ANCIENT AND MODERN

About thirty kilometres from Dublin, a traveller going north-west on the Navan road through the rolling, low-lying pastures of Meath, could well pass the Hill of Tara without noticing it. The hill is a low ridge, running north and south, to the left of the road. The driver may notice on the high ground that forms the western skyline a commonplace clump of trees round an old church tower. This is unremarkable. A similar ridge forms the eastern skyline, with a slightly more impressive but ruinous tower — the Hill of Skreen. From the main road there is nothing noteworthy about either.

Each hill has its story, but the story of Tara is one to stir any imagination. Imagination will be needed on a visit to the Hill, for there is little to be seen that will mean much except to the instructed eye of the archaelogist. Yet it is worth a visit.

Several by-roads to the left lead up towards the ridge. One gives access over a stile to the grassy slope quite near the crest. The short walk up reveals several grass-grown mounds against the sky. Then, at the top, as the ground begins to fall away steeply on the far side, a vast expanse of country opens out below, to the west, the central lowlands of Ireland extending away into blue distances. The eye can just make out on far horizons the dim outlines of the hills that rim the plain, in all four provinces. To the south, beyond Dublin, are the Wicklow hills and other Leinster mountains; to the north the Cooleys and Mournes on the Ulster borderlands and, more remotely, the mountains of mid-Ulster; and far, far away in clear weather, the Munster Galtees can be seen to the south-west and, in the west, the mountains of Connemara in distant Connacht. It is a king's view over the plain. This was a royal site.

One of the mounds on the middle of the ridge, flat-topped and surrounded by a ditch and outer bank, is surmounted by a cast concrete statue of St. Patrick. He is portrayed anachronistically, dressed in late medieval bishop's garb. The statue is in a state of dilapidation, and will no doubt not last much longer; which is as well, for it is a crude, vulgar and ugly piece of work. Beside it, within an iron-fenced enclosure, there stand also a tablet with an inscription commemorating the insurgents of Meath and nearby counties who were cut down on the Hill by regular troops on a summer day in 1798, and a round-tipped standing stone.

Here is a good place to begin to unravel the tangled skein of legend and history that is connected with Tara. For the advent of St. Patrick in Ireland marks the point at which we begin to move from the archaeologist's history of nameless peoples and from the mists of legend and myth into the history based on what was written down at the times we are studying.

The statue on Tara commemorates an episode of legend, not history. But Patrick was an historical figure who lived in the fifth century of our era. His arrival is not quite the first documented episode of our history. That was the arrival of another bishop, Palladius, who was sent by Pope Celestine in 431 to be 'the first bishop of the Irish Christians'. Some hundreds of years earlier however, there was a non-event, also documented at the time, which, oddly enough, is of great importance for understanding the development of early Ireland. This happened — or more accurately didn't happen — late in the first century. The Romans had recently conquered Britain and included it as a province in their imperial system. The governor of the province, Agricola, contemplated adding Ireland to the empire too. He made reconnaissance and assembled forces on the British coast facing the low-lying Irish coast that is only a few miles from Tara. Then he was distracted by other problems, in the north of Britain, and abandoned his Irish enterprise. The Roman legions never came.

That was a momentous non-event. Alone in the west, Ireland remained outside the great empire that for four centuries provided a centralised administration, with great cities, roads, bridges, aqueducts, postal services, publishing houses, tax officers and a regular and highly efficient military system over Europe from Scotland to the Sahara, from the Atlantic to the Euphrates. In Ireland, the way of life of the Iron-Age Celts continued.

But through those four centuries the influence on Ireland of the civilisation whose cities and villas lay only a hundred kilometres away across the Irish Sea, was considerable and continuous. On Tara itself there was evidence of this. A complex earthwork, lying towards the northern end of the ridge and named by fanciful medieval antiquaries 'the Rath of the Synods', has been excavated. It is the type of earthwork known in Ireland as a 'rath' or 'ring-fort' (usually a house-enclosure) but more elaborate than most, with four concentric banks and ditches. It appears to have had a complex history too, between the second century and the fourth, being used at different periods, it could seem, for habitation, ritual and burial.

There was evidence that the people living at Tara in this period were in communication with the Roman Empire, both by way of trade (there was pottery as well as some other Roman imports) and by correspondence (a Roman seal-box was found). The question is: who were the people living on the Hill?

A great body of medieval literature would persuade us that they were high kings of Ireland and their households. According to one of the many legends that grew around St. Patrick, for example, he landed on the nearby east coast on his mission to bring the Christian faith to Ireland. He camped on Slane, a hill overlooking the Boyne which is visible from Tara, and there lit a fire in the night to celebrate the beginning of the Easter festival, as it was that time of year. But this contravened the law, for Easter coincided with a pagan festival, and it was the rule that no fire must be lit in Ireland that night until the chief druid at Tara had first lit the celebratory pagan fire.

The symbolism of the story is simple and obvious. Patrick lit the light of the new faith. The story goes on to tell how he came to Tara, miraculously escaping from ambushes and stratagems of the high-king and his druids. Then, on the Hill itself, in the presence of the high-king Laoire, he engaged in a contest of magic (which of course he won) with the druids. Laoire, although refusing to become a Christian himself, reluctantly permitted Patrick to go on with his preaching, and the saint to convert the whole of Ireland.

Tara was chosen as the setting for this fable because of its prestige and importance in early Ireland. Modern scholarship has tried to get behind the accumulation of medieval legend, and has begun to reveal a quite different story, but one which is more interesting. Tara was a special, or sacred site of some kind for more than two thousand years before Patrick's time. Neolithic farmers used the hilltop, and well before 2000 BC they built and used a small megalithic tomb of the passage type there (perhaps more than one, but only one has been excavated so far). Many centuries later, in the Bronze Age, people of wealth and importance were buried on the Hill. The megalithic tomb is marked by the mound which the medieval storytellers fancifully called 'the Mound of the Hostages' (and of course there is a story to explain the name). It and several other earthworks (including the rath on which St. Patrick's statue stands) are all enclosed within the sweep of a great, roughly circular ritual ditch, with outer bank, that encompasses a large part of the hilltop.

The legendary name of the great enclosure is 'the Rath of the Kings'. It is probably of Bronze or of Iron-Age date and resembles a well-known type of earthwork known to archaeologists as a 'hill-fort' — except that in a hill-fort the boundary is defensive and there is an inner bank and an outer ditch.

Throughout the early historic period, to the twelfth century, the kingship of Tara was recognised as one of the most powerful in the country. Scholars no longer believe that in the earlier centuries there were 'high-kings of Ireland'. It would appear that in the whole island there were about 150 'kingdoms' (more accurately described perhaps, in cultural anthropological terms at least, as 'chiefdoms'). But these were loosely grouped under over-kings, who had some sort of dominance over their less powerful fellows. The Irish word for the largest of such groupings means literally 'fifth' (i.e. a fifth of Ireland) but the English equivalent usually used is 'province'. There were, in historic times, more than five 'fifths', or provinces, and since the Middle Ages only four are recognised, Ulster, Munster, Leinster and Connacht. The fifth which has disappeared was the middle (*Mide*, from which we have the county names Meath and Westmeath). The provincial royal centres were hilltop sites — Tara, in Meath, Cruachan, in what is now Co. Roscommon, in Connacht, Cashel (Co. Tipperary) in Munster, Emhain Macha (Co. Armagh) in Ulster, and, farther north still, Ailech (Co. Donegal) which functioned after dyunastic fortunes had changed and Emhain had declined, and Ailinn, in Leinster.

How exactly these royal sites functioned is uncertain. Irish society, at the time of St. Patrick and for a while later, was rural, without towns. The petty kingdoms, or chiefdoms, seem to have been based on an early tribal system, but by the fifth century this was already developing into more complex organisation. Society was stratified: each person had a designated grade or rank. However, it was not a society of individuals. The important unit, for property-holding and many legal matters, was the kin-group, and there were fine legal distinctions concerning degrees of kinship. The upper ranks of society counted their wealth in cattle, and their power in numbers of clients (people who owed them service or loyalty in return for 'loans' of wealth). Wealth, power and status were closely, although not rigidly, connected.

Within each kingdom there were royal kin-groups, from whom the new king would be chosen. Power, measured in clients, played a large part in the choice, and the royal kin-groups were turbulent, with many succession-disputes and feuds. Kingship, or at least provincial kingship, seems in pre-Christian times to have been largely sacral, or ritual. The king was intermediary between his people and what was outside them, whether human allies or enemies, or the forces of nature or the supernatural. He must be without physical blemish. Good weather, fecund herds and healthy crops were the signs of a good king, who observed the ritual requirements and prohibitions and taboos of his office.

At Tara, at the dawn of history, there was a ceremony called the *féis*, which happened in the reign of each successive king. Its precise nature is obscure, but it appears to have been an inauguration ceremony which embodied the notion that the king was mated to the goddess of sovereignty. Gerald of Wales, who came to Ireland at the end of the twelfth century with the Normans, tells an old story which he picked up in the country about pagan inauguration ritual in the north. There, he was told, it had been the custom for the new king to mate with a mare, whose flesh was then boiled into a broth which he drank. At Tara, the inauguration may well have involved some ceremony related to the sovereignty goddess Maeve (Medb), the same who figures as queen of Connacht in the saga *Táin Bó Cuailgne*. Her name is closely associated with the Hill, and at the southern end of the ridge there is a regular hill-fort which the medieval antiquaries named the Rath of Maeve.

Of the Roman influence on this society the most important was Christianity. It would seem that Christians were already numerous enough in the country by 431 for the first bishop, Palladius, to be appointed to them. But we know little of him or of many other fifth-century bishops who worked in Ireland. Patrick is the exception. He left writings which we can still read. He was a Roman Briton who as a boy was carried off in an Irish raid on Britain (such raids were frequent in the declining days of the empire) and spent some years as a slave in Ireland, as a herd. He escaped, but after many years returned to Ireland as a missionary bishop. His chief church was at Armagh, just beside the old royal site of Emhain Macha. He became the most famous of the British and Gaulish bishops of the time (the real Patrick all but vanishing beneath a huge accumulation of legend) and his church at Armagh came to be accepted as the chief church in Ireland: it is still the primatial see.

But within a few centuries the management of church affairs in Ireland had passed from the hands of bishops. The enthusiasm for monasticism reached western Europe from the deserts of Egypt and Syria and swept Ireland. This movement was founded on the impulse to withdraw from the world with its temptations and its many unchristian traditions and customs, and in remote places lead a life of prayer, fasting and mortification. The monasteries which became very numerous in Ireland were like villages or towns often founded on islands or in bogs or woods in the no-man's-land between petty kingdoms. They were inhabited by men or women who followed strict rules of life laid down by one or other leader of the monastic movement. Bishops often lived in the monasteries, but the head of the monastery was usually a priest without episcopal orders.

Irish buildings of the time were almost all of wood, and there are now no vestiges left above ground of timber buildings of this period. We can get some impression of the layout of an early monastery, however, from one or two examples in the windswept and treeless coastal areas, where building was in stone.

The best example is on the Great Skellig rock, thirteen kilometres off the south-west coast. The rock is pyramid-shaped and rises more than two hundred metres from the ocean. It and the nearby Little Skellig are inhabited by tens of thousands of sea-birds, including puffins and gannets. Like the sea-birds a small colony of monks nested on its crags in the seventh century. Nearly two hundred metres above the sea that breaks into restless foam all around the Rock, they built on a ledge half-a-dozen beehive-shaped huts and two tiny oratories. The structures were built without mortar, but of snugly fitted stones, and were well cladded with peaty sods of the sea-pink that forms spongy mats of vegetation in the gullies of the rock and on the ledges. In a little graveyard lie eight or nine generations of monks, each with a roughly shaped or incised cross to mark his place. In the centre of all a great slab of stone stands, simply shaped to a cross, and over the doorways of the now empty but still intact dwellings the same symbol of Christianity is picked out in stones of white quartz.

Ascetic simplicity is the motif of Skellig; but some of the great monasteries of mainland Ireland grew to be cities in which much secular business was transacted as well as spiritual. The civilization of Ireland in the seventh, eighth and nine centuries of our era was extraordinary. It had borrowed freely from the Roman and the post-Roman world, but it had escaped the externally imposed imperial discipline as well as the Woolworths or Brummagem material culture that brought an entropic monotony to every corner of the vast empire. Its disciplines were internal and sprang from powerful drives that are now, in a wholly different world, very difficult to understand.

That civilization had all the marks of a high and refined culture, and we are only now beginning to understand it, dimly. Above all it had the mark of assured, exquisite and perfect *confidence* in handling (through art and no doubt through life) the complex relationships of humanity, God and nature. It was an intensely religious culture, but it is imbued with the pagan tradition and under the surface of an austere Christian faith there is a burgeoning pantheism. Its philosophers display the profound scepticism (akin to the Eastern concept of the world as illusion) that has ever since been a characteristic of the distinctive Irish mind. Its lyric poetry alone forms one of the great literatures of the world.

We are fortunate to possess, the wrack of stormy centuries, a handful or two of works produced in that distant and mysterious world. A few texts survive, and we can see that by the seventh century Christianity had been both accepted and absorbed and metamorphosed by the culture of the Iron-Age Irish. Gold- and copper-smiths worked for kings and churchmen, producing sometimes ecclesiastical vessels or personal ornaments that display consummate skills and are on a par with the very best works produced by Kentish or Lombard jewellers of the time. The scribes developed a beautiful book-hand, so clearly legible that its influence has prevailed to the present day. The very type-face in which this is printed is partly derived from it. And some of the manuscripts are painted with extraordinarily elaborate — and often extraordinarily minute yet perfectly executed — ornament. By the end of the eighth century sculptors were beginning to create a Romanesque before its time, not in the design of churches but in the carving of great free-standing monuments, high crosses with bold reliefs of abstract patterns or figured scenes arranged in orderly compositions.

But as we move towards the Romanesque, the civilization begins to lose some of its originality of spirit as well as some of its élan. At most of the monastic sites where monuments survive today, it is stone buildings and works of this later period that we see. They illustrate the civilization in its maturity, when it was still active, innovative, inventive, forming closer cultural links with Carolingian and Romanesque Europe. But it is the earlier, seventh and eighth centuries, that are rightly termed 'the golden age'.

Throughout these centuries Tara, it is likely, was as grass-grown as it now is, uninhabited and open to the sky. Its true meaning was religious and pagan. The triumph of Christianity involved its desertion. But its prestige and significance remained. To hold Tara was a symbolic necessity for the kings who would be paramount in the northern half of Ireland, and by the eighth and ninth centuries its possession was becoming associated with the emerging concept of the high-kingship of all Ireland.

By then Christianity and kingship had long come to terms; the church was working hand in hand with the more powerful kings in the process of state formation. And the Irish church had expanded. Beginning in the sixth century, quite soon after the first development of monasticism, swarms of monks began to go into exile overseas on 'pilgrimage for Christ' — a form of penitential exercise. One of these, Columba, of royal blood, founded a monastery on the little island of Iona, off the west of Scotland, just beyond the boundaries of an expanding Irish colony that had been established from Ulster in Argyllshire. Iona became a centre of great ecclesiastical and political importance. In 574 Columba 'ordained' Aidan as king of the Irish colony — Dal Riada — which was eventually to grow into the medieval kingdom of Scotland. Columba's successors were to cooperate with kings of Northumbria, in northern England, in the conversion of the Anglians. Later, other Irish churchmen are found as resident scholars at the courts of Merovingian and Carolingian kings on the Continent.

But the independent tradition of pre-Christian Ireland was maintained, and was cherished by the poets and the jurists whose own position derived from it. For them Tara was a potent symbol. A thousand years later, when the Gaelic order finally collapsed under the pressures of the modern world, it had acquired added significance as the symbol of vanished ancient glory. After a period of bitter conflict and more bitter defeat, a poet in the seventeenth century wrote:

Do threascair an saol, 'sdo shéid an ghaoth mar smál

Alastrann, César, 'san méid sin do bhí ina bpáirt;
Tá Teamhair ina féar, agus féach an Traoí mar atá;
'Sna Sasanaigh féin: b'fhéidir go bhfaighdís bás.

The world has overthrown, the wind has blown as dust
Alexander, Caesar and their retinue;
Tara is grass; look at the state of Troy;
Perhaps the English themselves might die.

And that symbol persisted, century after century, while the countryside around Tara was changed and changed again. The broad grazing lands of the east, where Tara rises to the winds that blow across the breadth of Ireland, are the Irish equivalent of Britain's 'lowland zone': open to incoming peoples and trends. Here the Christian church was early established. Bishops' churches and, after a century or so, early monasteries were once numerous in the lowlands, widespread on the plains of Meath and Kildare, clustering thickly among the bogs and woods and gravel ridges of the south midlands, westward to the Shannon and beyond.

The few fragments that remain in some places do little justice to the great ecclesiastical population that once occupied the land. But here and there a slender tall round tower draws the eye across the landscape, or a sculptured high cross shows us the art of a wholly vanished world.

Much more impressive are the monuments to the life of the upper orders of lay people in early Ireland, the 'raths' or 'forts' which, even after huge destruction in recent decades are still very numerous. A century ago there were about 50,000 of them still more or less intact. A rath is an earthen enclosure, usually roundish, marked by a raised bank with an external ditch. Both bank and ditch are gapped, by an entrance causeway across the fosse leading in through an interruption in the bank. The interior of the rath is sometimes on a level with the surrounding land, sometimes raised, platform-like, to a higher level.

The raths were the farmsteads of the early historic period, where the people who owned cattle and property lived, or kept their stock. More than a hundred have been excavated by archaeologists. The findings are reasonably consistent. As we see them now, they have been subjected to a thousand or more years of weathering since they were last in use. The bank has crumbled down, much of it into the ditch, so that the contours of both have been softened and blurred. Originally, the one would have been much higher, the other much deeper. The bank would have been faced or crowned with a stout timber palisade, or wooden wall. At the entrance there were gates. Inside the enclosure, in many raths, there was a dwelling house, also of timber, and subsidiary buildings. Sometimes there were no buildings; the enclosure then was probably used as a cattle pen.

From the texts we understand that more elaborate raths — which had more than one bank or rampart surrounding the central enclosure — were marks of high social rank. The social pattern they represent has a long history. The settlement pattern is of dispersed farmsteads, each in the middle of its owner's land. In many parts of the country, the later medieval successor of the lonely rath is the stone tower house, of four or five storeys, with its machicolated battlements and its attached walled 'bawn', or yard. But this in turn was succeeded, in later centuries, by the undefended country house in the middle of its demesne, or the 'strong' farmer's house, with a walled yard enclosing the barns, byres and dwelling, set in isolation among its own fields.

The village in Ireland is a separate and distinct development, and much weaker, as an element in the total social rural scene, than in neighbouring countries. There are, at that, two kinds of villages — estate villages, formed by landlords to house some of their labourers, or having a similar origin, and 'cluster' villages, or 'clachans', associated with infield-outfield (or 'rundale') cultivation and with communal effort and ownership and intimate and complex extended-family economic control. But what dominates the Irish landscape is the isolated farmstead in the middle of its fields. In a country which is, by west European standards, very thinly populated, this adds to the sense of space, emptiness and isolation. It leaves a mark on the national character.

Yet the Irish today are a mainly urban people. This is a recent development, dating from the present century. But somewhat earlier Irish emigrants had developed their own urban style of life, in Liverpool, Glasgow, London, Boston, Montreal, New York, Philadelphia and other distant cities. This has left its mark on the character of other countries.

In Ireland itself, town life developed as an aspect of imported cultures. Christian monasticism gave rise to the growth of ecclesiastical cities as well as to the occupation of lonely and remote places by small ascetic communities of monks. In establishments like Clonmacnoise, Glendalough and Armagh there were populations of hundreds, perhaps sometimes even thousands. Some of these were monks or nuns, dedicated to a life of prayer and penance. But others were craftsmen, farmers, and their families, lay stewards who administered monastic property and possessions, scholars, traders, half-secularised ecclesiastical entrepreneurs, innkeepers and others who made a living from the exploitation of famous relics or the custody of shrines frequented by pilgrims. Some of the great metropolitan monasteries became so busy with such concerns that the truly devout among the religious seem to have moved away to retreats some little distance from the establishments to which they were attached.

Most such places have long returned to quiet — the peace of ruin and desertion. A few, like Kilkenny, Cork and Armagh, became the sites of

later medieval and modern towns. But, on the whole, it is the towns
resulting from another intrusive culture that have had the greatest success
in terms of survival. The Scandinavians who came to Ireland as raiders,
explorers and adventurers throughout the first half of the ninth century,
and who made considerable efforts in the second half of that century to
win land for settlement, in the early tenth century founded trading stations
around the coasts of the southern half of the island. These were the origin
of many of the principal cities of modern times — Dublin, Limerick,
Cork, Wexford and Waterford.

Ireland was ideally situated for one major branch of the long-distance
trade that revived in western and northern Europe in the ninth and tenth
centuries. The trade linked the northerly parts of Europe with North
Africa and the Mediterranean. The other major branch was in the east,
linking Sweden and Finland with Constantinople and the east
Mediterranean. There too Viking towns, such as Kiev, were founded, on
the banks of the great rivers. The Atlantic way led south through the Irish
Sea and by the coasts of France and Spain. 'Fare you south to Dublin: that
is the most famous route', said the saga. Walrus ivory, skins, slaves, silver
and other commodities and goods travelled by the route, and by the
eleventh century the trade was brisk and was having its widespread effects
on the territories it touched in passing.

In medieval times everywhere the contrast between town and country
was quite sharp. It was particularly so, perhaps, in Ireland, since the towns
were doubly foreign. Their people spoke a different language, quite
literally. And this continued in the later Middle Ages. For, while the
Scandinavian towns were, most of the time, subordinate to the native Irish
rulers of the hinterland, paying them tribute from the proceeds of their
trade, and often coming under their direct rule or supplying fleets or other
military service, they were superseded by a new urban system which stood
in a much less subservient relationship to the native polity.

The introduction, as mercenaries and adventurers, into Ireland in the
late twelfth century of Norman barons, knights and men at arms, led
within a generation to the takeover of much of Ireland by new landlords
and rulers. The kings of England claimed to be 'lords of Ireland' and their
agents functioned mainly through towns — the Scandinavian towns,
which they took over, and new towns which they founded.

In the medieval towns the language and traditions of England were
preserved and maintained through the Middle Ages. We can glimpse their
traces in a few places today — Kilkenny, Drogheda, corners of Galway, and
smaller places like Kilmallock, Adare, and Castledermot (for not all the
towns prospered and grew). There are outposts, too, great castles like
Trim or Carrickfergus, or urban-scale abbeys like Kells (Co. Kilkenny) or
Athassel. In these places we can trace, through architectural and sculptural

styles which pass from unmodified Early English to a highly distinctive and idiosyncratic late Irish Gothic, not a by-way but a high-road of Irish history. The grey stones, the Gothic black-letter on the tombs with their effigies and decorations, the square towers whose battlements survey a tamed countryside, all these register for us the colonial presence in medieval Ireland, a presence which became an integral and intimate part of Irish blood, bone and sinew, of field, pasture and wood, and, above all, of street and alley. Nowhere is more Irish than Kilkenny; nowhere in Ireland is more English, and Norman.

Every 'English town' of the Middle Ages and early modern times had its 'Irish town' attached, and its markets where country people and travellers came and went. In the town liberties an English-speaking Irish culture was nurtured for centuries before the Irish language in general began the great retreat that has lasted now for four hundred years. It is a culture coloured and marked both by the experience of the streets and taverns of urban life and by prolonged and close contact with the rural Gaelic world.

Even the later towns of the 'plantations' of Tudor and Stuart times came to develop something of a similar character. In theory, the government-sponsored plantations were attempts to replace the native population of various parts of the country, in whole or in part, by English or Scottish settlers introduced to provide a population amenable to English government, law and religion. In practice, even the most thoroughgoing plantations were incomplete. Newcomers arrived, to displace old landowners perhaps, but rarely to displace the whole working population of any region. Instead, they created simply a new element in the mosaic of settlement and culture. Since the descendants of planters were wholly dominant for a century and a half, and were, as they came to be known, the legally privileged 'Protestant ascendancy', the monuments of their long hegemony are numerous still in the land.

The most obvious survivals today perhaps are the Anglican churches, very very many of them nowadays disused, which have a distinctive character because so many were built, rebuilt, or modified during a period in the early nineteenth century when money for such work became available. The churches are obvious because they are by the main roads, often in the centres of towns or villages. In contrast, the Roman Catholic churches, different in style, commonly later in date, are frequently on the outskirts or wholly outside the centres of population — although they still attract large congregations, as they always did. This is a generalisation which is supported by numerous examples throughout most of the island; but in many parts of Ulster it breaks down. There, the churches of the presbyterians and other dissenting groups are commoner than the buildings of the Church of Ireland, and testify to a different religious pattern.

The houses of the Anglo-Irish ascendancy are only a little less obvious in the landscape than their churches. Everywhere in Ireland the stone walls of the landlords' demesnes survive patchily, although the estates for the most part have long been broken up. The breaking up was brought about, after much agitation and turmoil, by a series of land acts passed by British administrations at the end of the last century and the beginning of this. The cumulative effect of the acts was a major social revolution, from which the revolutionary politics of the early twentieth century can't be wholly separated. Pushed and prodded from below, the British government brought about a revolution from above which ended the dominance, and virtually ended the existence, of a highly distinctive colonial ruling class.

But, in the century and a half of their supremacy, the people of the ascendancy remodelled the face of Ireland. Their houses, big and small, were, like themselves, colonial in style — quite similar to their counterparts (of the appropriate period, the eighteenth and nineteenth centuries) in England, but with all sorts of quirky or unexpected differences in detail. Tudor and Jacobean mansions are comparatively few in Ireland — ruins, where they exist, or recent restorations, for the most part. Wars were being fought in Ireland throughout the sixteenth and seventeenth centuries, and it was only after the final defeat of James II by William III in 1691 that the country became peaceful and that governmental order could be extended throughout the island.

Large houses had of course been built during the long disturbed period before the final defeat of James II; but this event marks a real turning point. The Catholic landowners had supported causes which failed, and now there was a new order solidly established in the country. In the first half of the eighteenth century it set a new mark on the landscape through its large-windowed houses which expressed the domestic security and confidence of the owners and rulers of the land. Some of the grandest and most ambitious of the houses were built quite early in this period — Castletown, Co. Kildare, for example, with its great rectangular central block built about 1720, and its wings, linked to the centre by curved colonnades, built about ten years later.

The estates were laid out with avenues and ornamental plantations. Meanwhile, the farmland at this period was taking on the field-patterns, with hedgerows, that were to characterise it until the middle years of the twentieth century. Ireland, especially in its eastern parts, came to resemble Great Britain of the same period in its landscapes and architecture more closely than at any previous time.

It was a superficial resemblance. Ireland's economy continued to differ from England's. The difference was to increase as rapid economic change began to transform Britain. And the people of the Irish countryside — and of most of the towns — were different: Catholic, Irish-speaking, many of them, poor.

It became a land of stark contrasts in its society. And the contrasts grew. There was famine and plague in the seventeenth century. There was severe famine in the west in 1740. Then, for many decades, there was a remission of sorts. The population expanded until, by the end of the century, the people of the time, even with their inadequate and often misleading ways of counting, became both aware of the increase and concerned about it. Where there had been two million people in 1700, there were five million in 1800. To the statisticians and political economists of the time this was alarming: people were seen primarily not as hands to produce but as mouths to feed. And it was plain that in Ireland, as Ireland was run, so many mouths could not be fed. This circumstance, this perception, for two hundred years have been stamped on the Irish consciousness.

The rural patterns of the early eighteenth century came to be greatly modified, first by the demographic change involved in the huge increase in population — the total had exceeded eight million by the late 1830s — which created overcrowding and destitution in the poorer western areas, and then by the steady, dogged, often violent and bloody, advance of the mass of the population to full civil rights.

In the process the destitute and the poorest classes were virtually wiped out by famine, famine-related diseases, and migration. But Catholic tenant farmers and a Catholic mercantile and professional middle class fought their way to what was to be, ultimately, over most of the island, a politically, and in the long run economically, dominant position.

The makeshift shelters of the destitute, the rough structures of turves, have vanished from the face of the earth. The mud cabins of the poorer tenants have all but gone too. When the tenants became proprietors, in due course they came to have somewhat better dwellings. Land Commission cottages, built to one or two standard designs in the years around 1920, are still numerous in the countryside, but these in turn have largely been replaced by new bungalows. It is only the later stages of the emergence from mud hovels that are documented in rural buildings.

But it is the decade or so immediately after the second world war that saw the greatest recent transformation of rural Ireland. A major psychological change was brought about by the bringing of electricity to most parts of the country: the new source of power available for farm and domestic work also had an immediate effect on the social life of the countryside. In the same years there was a breakdown in the way of rural life that had become traditional since before the middle of the nineteenth century. The breakdown was most clearly marked by mass migration from the land. It was succeeded by the effects of a new economic policy and by ten years or so of comparative prosperity which was particularly marked in rural Ireland. This was the time when the Irish population ceased to be predominantly rural. The face of the country was changed as the towns expanded, each developing a ribbon-built sprawl of new cottages and bungalows from its outskirts along the main roads and by-roads around it. And the development of tourism and new, often transient, industries produced a great deal of other new buildings, while new methods and specialisations in agriculture altered the appearance of field and farm. The eighteenth- and early-nineteenth century patterns, while still clearly discernible, were beginning to give way to something new.

Many of these observations would apply to the whole island of Ireland. They are in large part responses to the changes taking place in the outside world. But there were and are some important differences in the north-east. The partitioning of Ireland in 1920 was a response to political differences within the island that derived from the settlement of large parts of Ulster, several hundred years earlier, by planters and migrants from Scotland and England who came then, and in later times, in sufficient numbers to give a distinctive character, especially to the eastern parts of the province. The distinctiveness was manifest in two principal ways. The proportion of Protestants, both Anglicans and Presbyterians, was much higher in the population than elsewhere in the island (a little over half, counting all Protestant denominations, in the province as a whole). And the industrial organisation of east Ulster at the end of the eighteenth century followed the northern British pattern, with factory production of cotton and linen cloth. By the late nineteenth century other industries had developed, in particular shipbuilding and various engineering trades, and Belfast had grown rapidly from being a small merchant town to become a large industrial city which had, by 1900, a greater population than Dublin.

This was chiefly a nineteenth-century development. It gives to much of Northern Ireland, especially in the eastern parts, a general appearance in its urban areas which resembles the appearance of the industrial north of England, or southern Scotland — although many differences can quickly be discerned by a second glance. It is essentially the appearance created by early industrial growth followed by subsequent decline. The peak of industrial activity and growth was passed before the Great War, and Ulster has been economically depressed for most of the time since then. But in the meantime, the decades of government spending in the United Kingdom after the Second World War have left their mark on Northern Ireland in the shape of a considerable physical infrastructure: roads, schools, hospitals, public housing, farms, all show the effects of grants, subsidies, subventions and direct public expenditure at levels considerably higher than those reached in the Republic across the Border. This is visible

An aerial view of Tara, Co. Meath

"The Mound of the Hostages", Tara, Co. Meath

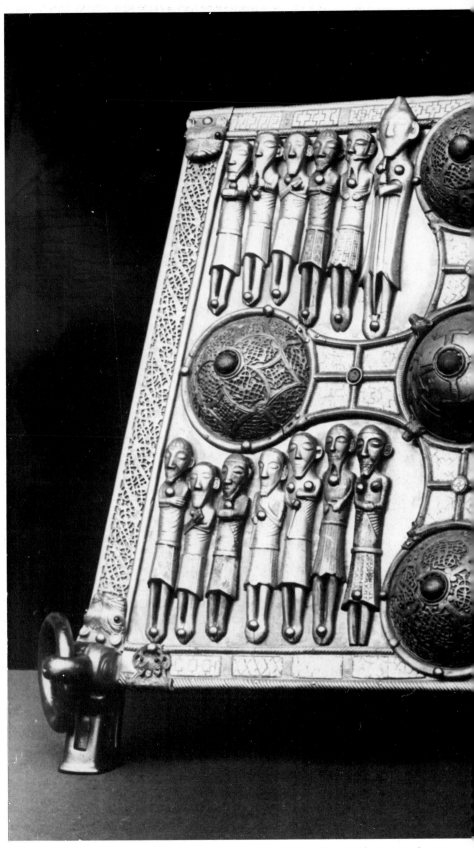

A reproduction of St. Manchan's Shrine in the Natio

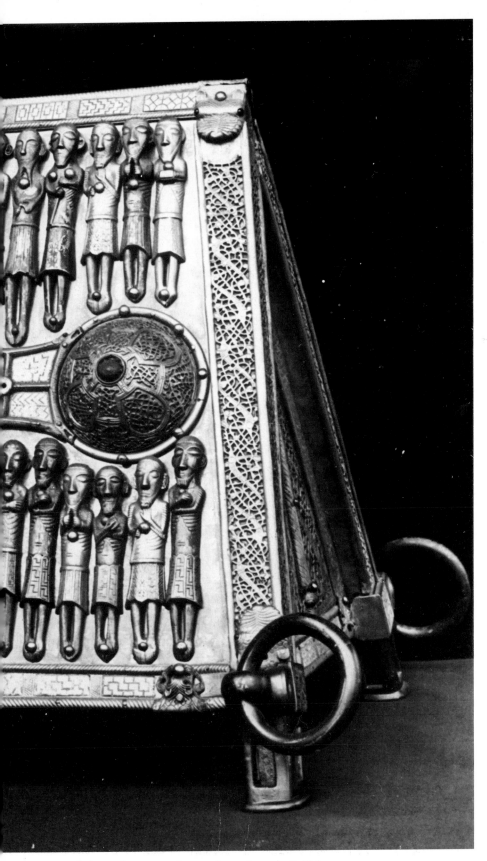

reconstructed from the original in Boher, County Offaly

Armagh seen from the Catholic Cathedral

The Great Skellig, Co. Kerry

in the landscapes and townscapes and, along with such details (now beginning to change on both sides of the Border) as red pillar-boxes in place of green, imposes on what was a very similar scene a difference created in a little over half a century.

But a countervailing change has worked in the other direction. New kinds of industrialisation, and other new activities characteristic of the twentieth century, such as the development of air transport, have occurred as much, or more, south as north of the Border. As a result, the late-nineteenth-century contrast between a modern industrialised east Ulster and a poor agricultural economy in the rest of the island has disappeared. East Ulster remains more densely populated than the country as a whole, but that balance too is changing. In this respect the chief contrast is between east and west. A chain of conurbations from Waterford to Larne houses the greater part of the island's population. Production *per capita* is much the same throughout Ireland. And the island has common problems: its politicians from both sides of the Border frequently find that they share an interest in dealing with the parliamentary and other institutions of the European Economic Community.

It is still possible, in a half-day's drive from almost any centre in Ireland, to see a remarkable number of archaeological monuments, representing almost every period of the past. The comparatively low density of population has combined with superstitious fear of 'fairy forts', thorny trees, and dwellings of the 'good people', and feelings of respect for the past, as well as a land-tenure system which discouraged all improvement, to preserve monuments of the past much better in Ireland than in most parts of western Europe. The old building was not demolished when the new was undertaken, but was left to fall into picturesque (or other) ruin. The rath in the corner of the field was not ploughed out, but was carefully avoided and left for cattle to graze. This has now changed. Bulldozers have overcome superstitious fears of interfering with ancient mounds and earthworks, land improvement grants have encouraged destruction of what doesn't fit the current season's fashion in agricultural methods, electricity has banished the fireside storyteller in favour of 'Dallas'. The twentieth century is depriving Ireland's archaelogical heritage of a great deal of material from earlier ages, but, perhaps by way of compensation, supplying instead a great quantity of concrete blocks and ornamental bricks for the investigations of archaeologists of the future.

5
DUBLIN

Almost a quarter of the population of all Ireland lives in or near Dublin. This is quite recent, but Dublin has had a considerable importance in Ireland for a very long time. At the beginning of the twentieth century, with about 300,000 people, it was smaller than Belfast, but it was the administrative centre of all Ireland. At the beginning of the nineteenth century, with about 100,000 fewer people, it was one of the chief cities of Europe, and by far the largest in Ireland, whose population then, however, was about the same as now.

Since 1900, in terms of the number of inhabitants and in many other ways, the relationship between Dublin and the rest of Ireland has changed very considerably. For example, for centuries it was chiefly through the medium of the Dublin-centred administration that English, or British, control and influence operated in Ireland. In the twentieth century Belfast became — but in quite a different way — the location of an equivalent link.

Most capital cities have ambiguous relations with their countries. So it is with Dublin. To begin with, it is not Irish in its foundation, and was not wholly Irish for a great part of its history, although — or perhaps because — it has been the seat of government for centuries. Until 1922 the government was English. Dublin Castle was the centre of the English administration in Ireland.

But the foreignness of Dublin goes further back. The Liffey is a small river which flows eastward into a magnificent bay whose embrace is addressed to Wales and England beyond the Irish Sea. This bay has probably been frequented for thousands of years by visitors from Britain and from farther afield to the east. In the ninth century Viking fleets sailed in, fought among themselves, and established a base from which raids inland were mounted. In the tenth century the Scandinavians established a permanent trading town on the south bank of the Liffey near its mouth and close to the ford by which a main north-south route crossed the stream.

Excavations conducted by the National Museum at Wood Quay and High Street have revealed the wooden buildings — houses and workshops — and the boarded alleyways and sidewalks of the town. The palisades that enclosed the city were, it seems, advanced several times to allow for expansion, until a city wall was constructed in stone in the eleventh century.

High Street runs along a low ridge, parallel to the south bank of the river. The Scandinavians — 'Ostmen', as they came to be known — built a small cathedral, Christchurch, at the eastern end of the street. It was rebuilt by the Anglo-Normans in the late twelfth century, and, after many subsequent rebuildings, it still stands. The Scandinavians had first appeared on the Irish coasts at the end of the eighth century — the earliest record is from 795 — when they raided the coastal island of Lambay, just north of Dublin Bay. For about fifty years they appeared sporadically, occasionally foraging inland. They were mostly Norse, from the fjords in the region of Bergen and Stavanger. About the middle of the ninth century they began to organize fleets and to mount expeditions whose chief object, it would seem, was the winning of land for settlement.

In this their success was very limited, but the Dublin base developed connections with the more successful settlement enterprises in the Isle of Man and parts of northern England and the Isles. When, in the tenth century, a more mixed group of Scandinavians (including many from the western Viking colonies, Iceland, the Isles and elsewhere) began to found trading towns round the south and south-east of Ireland, at Limerick, Cork, Waterford, Wexford and Dublin, they added to the number of petty states in the Irish political system, and also added something new.

They had a major impact on Irish society, not through political or military power, but by developing a gradual re-orientation, particularly of the whole south-eastern half of the country. Their trading towns were small colonies. They were also way-stations in a long-distance trade. They maintained fleets and kept a close and continuous connection with Britain. After the Norman conquest of England, this connection assumed new importance, all the more so since the Ostman towns had by then complex economic and cultural relations with the major Irish kings, to whom they were politically subordinate within Ireland. By the late eleventh century, Dublin, by then a busy centre of trade, communications and craft production, was the chief Ostman state involved in this activity and in these relations.

A century later, Dublin, like the other Scandinavian towns, became a prize to be won in the complicated manouevrings that ensued after the deposed king of Leinster, Diarmait mac Murchada, recovered his kingdom with the aid of land-hungry Norman barons and knights from Wales. Diarmait made his allies' leader, the earl of Striguil, known as Strongbow, his heir; others set about winning lands for themselves. When the then king of England, Henry II, intervened to control the activities of his barons, he invoked a papal grant of a 'lordship' of Ireland, which he had obtained some years before, crossed the Irish Sea in 1171, and held court in a specially erected wattle pavilion at Dublin. The Ostmen had been defeated in battle, and the Dublin fleet had sailed away. Henry granted the city to its chief trading partner, the city of Bristol.

The intervention of the king of England reversed the process of political unification which had just about reached completion at the time. Throughout the Middle Ages the lordship functioned through great magnates descended from the first generations of Norman settlers. These functioned as much by diplomacy as much as by the exercise of proxy authority in a fragmented polity.

But, after a fashion, English rule continued, often very limited in its territorial scope. The Scandinavian towns, as well as some of later foundation, were its centres, and of these Dublin remained the most important. It was the centre of the territory extending for about fifty miles along the east coast and less than thirty miles inland which remained in settled obedience to English law. This territory was protected by a linear earthwork on the landward side, to discourage raiders and cattle-reavers, and was known from it as 'the English Pale'. Dublin was the heart of the Pale, and the heart of Dublin was the Castle, the stone fortress of the early thirteenth century that was the direct successor of Henry II's pavilion. For seven and a half centuries the Castle was the symbol of English power in Ireland.

Medieval Dublin was a small walled town running along the ridge. A bridge spanned the Liffey before it widened out to the bay, and the city spread across the river with the growth on the north bank of the Ostmantown, whose name was later corrupted to Oxmantown. Downstream, on either shore, there were great medieval abbeys, with their buildings, gardens and orchards. These were suppressed in the Reformation, but the site of one, lying to the east of the main city, was used for the foundation of a university by Queen Elizabeth I in 1592. Dublin University had, and has, only one college, Trinity. Inland, to the west, there were also extensive monastic lands outside the city walls. One of the monastic estates, north of the river, was to be developed later as the Phoenix Park, a great expanse of gardens, playing fields and woods which, in the present century, has been surrounded by the expanding city.

Dublin today is not very rich in medieval remains, at any rate, not above ground. A great wealth of foundations of timber structures was revealed by the National Museum's excavations of the Viking and early Norman city in the 1970s, but these have now vanished under the arrogant brutalist blocks of the city offices. No houses of the Middle Ages now survive, and much less than might be expected of defensive structures, or even church buildings. Dublin was wholly remodelled in the late seventeenth and early eighteenth centuries, as the capital of a proud colonial nation.

A few medieval buildings, mostly extensively rebuilt, survive, however, and these are mostly churches. Irish cathedrals in general are small, compared with those of many other places, but St. Patrick's Cathedral in Dublin, more than three hundred feet long and the largest of Ireland's medieval churches, is, even in its partly rebuilt and restored state, a major monument of the English Pale.

It is also somewhat more, since it seems certain that the church of 'St. Patrick de Insula' was erected on a spot, outside the thirteenth-century walls, where a pre-Norman church stood by a holy well. The site appears to have had some traditional, if highly dubious, association with St. Patrick. The early building standing there may well have been of wood, as so many structures were, but nothing remains of it. However, in 1901, when works were in progress at the cathedral, a stone carved with a ringed cross was found in excavations near the west tower. It was taken to mark the position of the well.

For most people one of the most interesting questions about St. Patrick's is why it should be a cathedral at all, when Dublin had another and earlier cathedral, Christ Church — which, moreover had the advantage of standing in or near the middle of the little city, within the walls. The situation is not unprecedented and has occurred elsewhere, although not usually in so glaringly obvious a fashion, in connection with medieval disputes and quarrels. Christ Church had been founded in the eleventh century and was the bishop's church of Norse Dublin. When the Normans took over in the late twelfth century it had a regular chapter of Arrouasian canons and was therefore monastic in its establishment. It was also Irish in the character and membership of its chapter, and in general was contrary to the character which the English church of the time favoured.

The first Norman archbishop, John Comyn, failed in his efforts to dislodge the Arrouasian canons and to obtain the kind of full control that he wanted over the cathedral. It was he who established a church, not originally of cathedral status, but with a chapter of secular canons, outside the walls to the south, in 1191. This became a cathedral church in 1213, and a new building, on a scale to match this distinction, was begun some years later by Archbishop Henri de Londres. The new cathedral was consecrated in 1254, although not all the work on it had then been completed. Parts of its fabric still survive in the present structure.

St. Patrick's as it stands today, however, is, more than most ancient churches, a patchwork of many periods. Its exposed position outside the walls of the medieval city was not to its advantage, even though John Comyn and his successor Henri de Londres provided for its defence by building a castle (later the palace of St. Sepulchre) beside the church. But when the citizens of Dublin set about protecting the city as Edward Bruce's Scottish and Irish army marched towards it in 1316, they burned St. Patrick's as well as other structures outside Dublin's walls. This was by no means the only misfortune suffered by the fabric. In the same year, 1316, part of the north-west tower fell, and further extensive fire-damage was caused in 1362. Archbishop Minot built the present tower in 1381 as part of the reconstruction made necessary by this fire, but there were later destructions and dilapidations in the history of the building, until two extensive nineteenth-century restorations made it fully fit for use again for the first time since the late Middle Ages.

Similar stories can be told of many old buildings, epitomizing a wider history. St. Patrick's, like the nearby Christ Church, is a building in which today, because of restoration, one is as conscious of the nineteenth as of the thirteenth century. There is something dead about Victorian reconstruction Gothic, and in St. Patrick's this combines with a severe austerity in the original design to give an impression of coldness, at least on first acquaintance. In spite of this severity, and of the overwhelmingly 'restored' impression it gives at first glance, the cathedral remains a handsome and impressive church. It is very different from the products of the architectural tradition of pre-Norman Ireland; very English, or colonial-English, in its spirit and feeling. But this is as it should be, because that is what the cathedral of medieval Dublin represents: the English colony in Ireland, a solid and inescapable part of Irish history. The monuments of that colony, apart from their intrinsic merits, serve to remind us of the complexity of the past.

Henry II's Lordship of Ireland derived from a papal grant, embodied in the bull *Laudabiliter* issued by the only English Pope, Hadrian II. There is no doubt that, by the twelfth century, the Irish seemed very out of line to the people who were busy re-organizing western Europe at the time, in spite of earlier Irish contributions to European Christianity, and in spite of the reputation which the Irish had earlier enjoyed for learning and sanctity. Most twelfth-century comment is adverse, sometimes extremely so. The Irish church system was both archaic and aberrant.

Irish society, influenced by Roman customs through the church but never moulded by Roman conquest, seemed even more archaic than the church, with its retention of so much from the prehistoric Celtic Iron Age. The inter-personal and inter-family relationships of the Irish formed a social and political tissue whose texture was quite different from that of the societies now dominating western Europe. The formidable groups of military organization-men who so colourfully and effectively made their appearance on the Irish scene in the late twelfth century were adaptable. But their attempts to conquer and organize Irish kingdoms tended to be rather like the British attempts in the early nineteenth century to conquer the Ashanti — misdirected through a constant misreading of the symbols valued and honoured by the opposed culture. Ignorant armies, as so often, clashed by night.

The king's intervention was a kind of crusade. Irish Christianity had come to seem so odd that it was hardly regarded, by the more intolerant exponents of the new order in the western church, as Christianity at all. The age was almost as unwilling to tolerate differences in practice as differences in dogma, and hardly distinguished between them. Their marriage customs caused the Irish to be regarded as incestuous; their ordinations of clergy and consecrations of bishops were held to be irregular; their liturgy did not conform. In the 'church reform' of the eleventh and twelfth centuries we can discern the familiar prejudiced face of imperialism.

It is true that there had been a reform movement in the Irish church too. This had been stimulated by the independent actions of Dublin and the other Ostman towns in the eleventh-century, influenced by the empire-building of the archbishops of Canterbury after the Conquest, but sponsored ultimately by leading Irish kings and churchmen. However, the reorganization carried out by the reformers undoubtedly was undergoing a great deal of backsliding by the late twelfth century as old interests reasserted themselves. The new bishop, with his diocese, tended to be the old monastic *comharba* with his *paruchia*, in barely changed guise. The new Cistercian abbeys (of which St. Mary's in Dublin, on the north bank of the Liffey, was one of the greatest) were already reverting to type and taking on again the characteristics of the old Irish monasteries. Above all, what was wrong with the Irish in some European eyes was that they did not conform to the new and vast centralized organization that was being established in Christendom.

A strange process of acculturation took place as a result of the Norman settlement, but although there was fairly dense colonization in some areas, such as south-east Leinster, the Gaelic world remained unassimilable throughout the Middle Ages. 'Crusades' continued to be necessary, and by the sixteenth century Ireland was even more alien in English eyes than it had been in the twelfth century. To the Elizabethans, the Irish in their forests and bogs were almost as strange as the Amerindians in the woods of Virginia. But in early modern times the Gaelic world was virtually destroyed, and was replaced by an English-speaking Ireland of very different character.

In the meantime, Dublin was the principal base in which English Government, law, speech and manners were preserved, but the city was at times close beset. The protected (although often raided) territory of the Pale extended northwards and inland from the walls, but on the south the Wicklow hills reached the bay, and beyond the meadows south of the city walls, across the turbulent and unbridged Dodder stream, the land was open to the Irish of the wooded glens and mountain fastnesses. The city, like other English towns, paid 'black rent' — protection money.

An illuminated page from the Book of Kells, Trinity College, Dublin

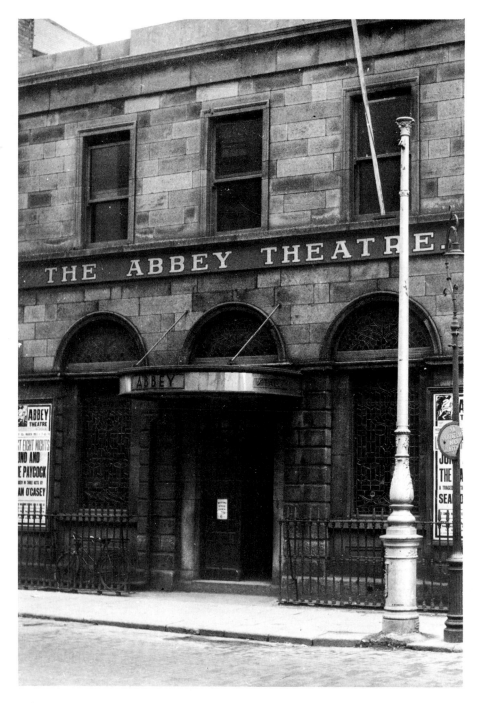

The old Abbey Theatre Dublin.

A fireplace, Florencecourt, Co. Fermanagh

View of Trinity College and College G

n (c. 1760–1803), *National Gallery*

Portrait of William Butler Yeats by J. B. Yeats

'Irish Soldiers', a drawing by Albrecht Dürer

Irish solders from the United Nations Peacekeeping Force in the Lebanon

Seán Ó Faoláin

In 1541 Henry VIII took the title 'King of Ireland'. He and his Tudor successors, his three children Edward, Mary and Elizabeth, during the remaining years of the century reduced Ireland piecemeal to submission. This involved wars of conquest which, at times and in places, had the character of wars of extermination.

The English conquest of Ireland coincided with the Reformation. Henry's discarding of papal authority and his suppression of the monasteries were acceptable in Ireland, but the doctrinal and liturgical changes brought about under Edward provoked a strong reaction among the long-established colonists in Ireland and set them at odds with the officials and agents who were coming over in increasing numbers from England. This division between the 'New English' and the 'Old English' initiated a political problem that was to persist for another hundred years, through the civil wars that disturbed Ireland even more than Britain, and that ended in the triumph of the Protestant (or, roughly, 'New English') cause in Ireland.

Dublin retained its medieval shape through most of these wars, but after the Restoration, the Viceroy of the time, the Duke of Ormonde, initiated what was to be in effect the planning of a new and elegant capital city.

The confiscated monastic estates surrounding the medieval city provided the basis for expansion. Almost a century earlier, Queen Elizabeth had founded a Protestant university, whose buildings occupied the site of the monastery of All Hallows, immediately to the east of Dublin. Ormonde built new bridges on the Liffey and took in the lands just north of the river. He enclosed the old Templar property west of the city, forming what was to become the Phoenix Park north of the river, and the Royal Hospital to the south. The Royal Hospital, designed by Sir William Robinson, was the first of the monumental buildings of the city that was to take shape.

Expansion was rapid in the eighteenth century. Dublin was now the capital of a new, rich landowning and governing class, firmly established after the defeat of James II and of the Catholic nobility and gentry who had supported his cause. The new establishment was to be known as 'the Protestant Ascendancy'. Their Dublin replaced the medieval city. They had their own parliament, that of the kingdom of Ireland, which existed in Dublin until the last hour of the century.

Land was reclaimed from the estuary, and a body called the Commissioners for Making Wide and Convenient Streets supervised the laying-out of a splendid system of streets and squares. Builders put up rows of four-storeyed houses of brick, punctuated by occasional, grander stone-faced houses of the nobility. The parliament of the Anglo-Irish was subordinate until 1782, when they secured legislative independence from the British parliament. The Dublin parliament ceased to exist on January 1, 1801, as a result of the passing of the Act of Union of 1800, which created the United Kingdom of Great Britain and Ireland and gave Ireland representation in the Westminster houses of Lords and Commons instead of Dublin. But while Dublin functioned as the capital of the nation it grew to be one of the chief cities of Europe and it was adorned with splendid buildings.

The hub of the city was now some distance to the east of the medieval walled area, at Hoggen Green, now College Green. Here, by the end of the century, the handsome Palladian facade of the rebuilt Trinity College faced the colonnades of the nobly planned Houses of Parliament (which are now the Bank of Ireland). Downstream rose the tall dome of the great Custom House, which presided over the city's trade, while upstream, across the river from the medieval core of the city, another dome crowned the central block of the courts of justice, known as the Four Courts. Many other monumental buildings, on a slightly smaller scale, marked the streets and squares of a city which housed about a quarter of a million people by the end of the eighteenth century.

Eighteenth-century Dublin, therefore, was the monument of a ruling class. It remains, to a large extent, their monument. This was the class that Yeats, in his later writings and thoughts, was to exalt as one of the two pillars of his idealised traditional Ireland which he wished to see prevail (the other was the peasantry). In a famous speech to the Irish Free State senate, he described the members of that class as 'no petty people'. He brings their names into his poems: Swift, Berkeley, Goldsmith, Burke, Grattan. Their statues and memorial tablets adorn Trinity College, College Green, and the walls and chapels of the cathedrals. And, in spite of much destruction, in spite of much new building that is indifferent in quality, or worse, in the recently renewed expansion of the city, Dublin still takes much of its character from its eighteenth-century formation. This is specially true of the quieter squares and streets south of the river, in particular Merrion and Fitzwilliam squares. Within a regular and repetitive general scheme, most of the original facades, still preserved, show great variety of detail, especially in their doorways and fanlights.

Most of the twentieth-century sprawl extending deep into the countryside is fairly characterless; but the shape of inner Dublin is still, by and large, that given to it in the Georgian period. However, the rhythms and intervals of the eighteenth-century cityscape, reasonably courteously observed in the Victorian and Edwardian additions, are now abruptly interrupted by monuments on a larger scale, expressive of the power of money and of bureaucracy, both of the public and of the private varieties.

The Central Bank building in Dame Street dominates the vistas of that part of inner Dublin by its stocky and glooming mass, a ziggurat of the usurers. This and other works of Sam Stephenson (such as the city offices on Wood Quay) are impressive, designed with a commitment to see the visual idea through to its conclusion, and thorough in their detailing; but in their brutal assertiveness they seem to be out of touch with the Irish tradition in building.

Dublin's chief thoroughfare, the very broad O'Connell Street, formerly Sackville Street, has lost the elegance that once graced it, but retains the spaciousness that its great width and ample scale gave it. The monument that once dominated the street — being built to its scale — the 36-metre column that generations of Dubliners knew as 'Nelson's Pillar' — was blown up in 1966. Just beside it, the General Post Office designed by Francis Johnson early in the nineteenth century, was ruined by British shelling when it was occupied as insurgent headquarters in the 1916. This has been rebuilt.

The period of more than a century from the Union to 1916 was marked by a continually renewed struggle to overthrow the Ascendancy. This struggle, since the Ascendancy was backed by and associated with Great Britain, had from the beginning a nationalist character, but took a variety of different forms, against a background of discontent and sporadic violence. Ireland under the Union was, most of the time, all but ungovernable and was held in check by the passing of various 'coercion acts' and their implementation and by the deployment through the country not only of troops but of a paramilitary police force (the Royal Irish Constabulary) one of whose functions was the gathering, and steady supply to Dublin Castle, of political intelligence.

Dublin after the Union, then, was no longer the proud colonial capital it had been in the eighteenth century. Nor did it quite become a provincial 'national' capital, like Edinburgh or Cardiff: the Union, if ever it had any sweetness to offer the masses of people in Ireland, very soon went sour, and, in a country seething with discontent, Dublin was essentially an imperialist base.

Irish discontent had been swelling in the later eighteenth century, and, ironically, the Union had itself been an attempt to deal with it. The American revolutionary war had stimulated the Ascendancy in Ireland, while arming themselves in support of Great Britain in the war against, not only the disaffected Americans, but also France and Spain, at the same time to use their arms to achieve their own colonial independence. A convention of their Volunteers in Dungannon, Co. Tyrone, opened their campaign. It was followed through in the parliament in Dublin and in the streets outside, where the Volunteers paraded with a great show of force, to win legislative independence for the colony in 1782. But, ten years later, in the general upheaval in European political ideas associated with the

French Revolution, a much more radical independence came to be envisaged, and, it might be said that in the last decade of the eighteenth century the themes of modern Irish politics were first given full expression. The organisations known as the societies of United Irishmen were founded (and were strongest in their place of origin, Protestant east Ulster), initially aiming at radical parliamentary reform, but soon becoming revolutionary in intention, in organisation and in method, seeking complete separation from England and the establishment of an Irish republic.

The United Irishmen soon made contact with and drew wide support from Catholic rural organisations known as Defenders — rural secret societies of a kind that had been active since soon after the mid-century. The Defenders had become involved, especially in the Ulster borderlands, in a conflict with Protestant tenant farmers and labourers in the densely populated countrysides of south and mid-Ulster, where these classes, with the rise in rural numbers, found themselves in competition for livelihood. The Orange order was founded after a bloody clash between Catholic and Protestant gangs in Co. Armagh in 1795. It was Protestant (almost wholly Anglican at that time) and it supported the existing order against attempts to overthrow it.

The origins of Irish republicanism at that time, beginning in Belfast, have passed into the political consciousness of modern Ireland in ways which have distorted meaning. Of the two or three dozen leading figures of the United Irishmen, one has (with some reason) been singled out by those who would claim to be in their tradition: Theobald Wolfe Tone, a Dubliner.

Wolfe Tone is on one level a figure of myth, especially since Patrick Pearse in the twentieth century established a canon for the Irish republican tradition in which Tone was the fountainhead for the stream of pure doctrine which flowed down through the nineteenth-century mediators, Davis, Mitchel and Lalor.

This tradition is unhistorical. It places Tone, and the whole tangled episode of the 1798 uprisings, in the context not of their own time but of nineteenth-century romantic and conspiratorial nationalism. It absorbs them all indeed into Pearse's own political consciousness and into his fin-de-siècle part-literary, part-mystical fantasy of redemption by blood. The tradition is less republican than nationalist and separatist. It is not an inclusive but an exclusive tradition (as may be seen in the detailed history of republican splits), although it claims to seek the unifying of all Irish people. The unity of minds and hearts it has aimed at has something in common with Roman ecumenism before Vatican II: it involved the acknowledgment of truth by error.

On another level, which is reached as soon as his own writings are read with a clear mind, Tone is one of the least charismatic, least mythical and mystical of revolutionaries; human, fallible, ambitious but at the same time diffident in a way, pragmatic, imprudent, cheerful and likeable.

'Republicans' in the narrow recent sense can indeed find in Tone's writings what they seek. The sacred texts are there: 'To subvert the tyranny of our execrable Government, to break the connection with England, the never-failing source of all our political evils, and to assert the independence of my country — these were my objects: to unite the whole people of Ireland, to abolish the memory of all past dissensions, and to substitute the common name of Irishman in place of the denominations of Protestant, Catholic, and Dissenter — these were my means'. But there is a contrast between his magnanimous and light-hearted spirit and the puritanical earnestness of many who proclaim themselves his followers.

Like so many of his fellows in the United Irish clubs, Tone thought as a colonist who, partly from the example of America and partly from the teaching of revolutionary France 'discovered that he had a country'. The 'execrable government' was judged to be so on the basis of its actions rather than its pretensions, and that the connection with England was 'the never-failing source of all our evils' was inferred not from any dogma of Ireland's sacred and separate nationhood but from observation of current politics. Tone was an eighteenth-century man, living in the Age of Reason. His political ideas, right or wrong, were derived not from a mystique but by rational process.

He moved to a political extreme partly because he lived in terrible times when moderation could find little place. It was a contest, as he saw it and put it, between 'aristocracy' and 'the people': it was, in other words, the time of the French Revolution, and Tone's principles were Jacobin. His political ideas were not, perhaps, very profound, but they were soundly democratic. He believed in the *independence* of Ireland as a necessary means to achieving the *liberty* of its people, as individuals. He always distinguishes the two words, in this sense: he hardly envisages any abstract 'Ireland' as distinct from the people of the island, still less any concept of 'Ireland's freedom', and his priority is always for the individual's freedom. Tone was the type of the bourgeois revolutionary, content enough in acceptance of the contemporary values of his class, resentful of aristocratic and unearned privilege, humane and magnanimous, conventional in most of his sentiments.

On the question of property, crucial in examining the thought of any revolutionary, Tone is ambiguous. He writes in his Journal on April 27th: 'Why does England so pertinaceously resist our independence? Is it for love of us — is it because *she* thinks *we* are better as we are? That single argument, if it stood alone, should determine every honest Irishman. But, it will be said, the United Irishmen extend their views farther; they go now to a distribution of property and an agrarian law. I know not whether they do or no. I am sure that in June, 1795, when I was forced to leave the country, they entertained no such ideas. If they have since taken root among them, the Irish gentry may accuse themselves . . . If such men, in the issue, lost their property, they are themselves alone to blame, by deserting the first and most sacred of duties — the duty to their country. They have incurred a wilful forfeiture by disdaining to occupy the station they might have held among the People, and which the People would have been glad to see them fill; they left a vacancy to be seized by those who had more courage, more sense, and more honesty; and not only so, but by this base and interested desertion they furnished their enemies with every argument of justice, policy, and interest, to enforce the system of confiscation'.

His view of the Ireland of his time is cool, as set forth in his memorandum to the French government in 1796, proposing an invasion. He estimates the population at about four-and-a-half million persons (probably an under-estimate), 'of whom the Protestants, whose religion is the dominant one, and established by law, constitute four hundred and fifty thousand, or one tenth of the whole; the Dissenters, or Presbyterians, about nine hundred thousand, or one fifth (these are probably over-estimates); the Catholics form the remaining three million one hundred and fifty thousand.'

Of these he regarded the Protestants, the group which formed his own background, as being, by their interest 'devoted implicitly to the connection with England', and the Catholics as being, by theirs, 'trained from their infancy in an hereditary hatred and abhorrence of the English name, which conveys to them no ideas but those of blood and pillage and persecution'.

Of the three groups it is plain that he most highly esteemed the Dissenters who, he says, 'are from the genius of their religion, and the spirit of enquiry which it produces, sincere and enlightened republicans', and who had, he believed, been finally converted by the example of the French Revolution to principles which overcame their distaste for 'the Catholic natives, whom they detested as Papists and despised as slaves'.

While he sincerely hoped for the merging of the distinction between the three groups in 'the common name of Irishman', Tone did, as a matter of practice, envisage an alliance of Catholics and Dissenters against the English government, which meant in effect against the Irish Protestants too — since he had no hope of winning them over in advance of revolution. But after the establishment of independence he aimed at a union of the three in a new Ireland which would *not* be a revived medieval Gaelic society but a rationalistic secular state on the model of the French Republic. He failed; nor has his failure been diminished by all who claim to be his successors.

Tone's personal efforts to gain French help were quite successful. A major French expedition sailed for Ireland in 1796. It was scattered by storms and was unable to make a landing, although the British navy failed to intercept the French on either the outward or the return voyage. Two much smaller expeditions sailed in 1798, Tone with the second of them, which was intercepted and defeated in Lough Swilly. Tone, taken in French officer's uniform, was condemned to be hanged as a traitor. Unwilling to face this dishonourable death, rather than execution as a soldier, he killed himself in Dublin Castle.

But after 1796, the government had moved ruthlessly against the United Irish organisation and against those parts of the country where it had flourished. When uprisings occurred in different regions in 1798, they were uncoordinated and, in part, quite out of control of the United Irish planners. Popular armies fought the redcoats, and also took revenge on their immediate oppressors. In Wexford, tenant farmers staunchly faced professional soldiers, but mobs also butchered Protestants, who, through the penal laws against Catholics, had constituted themselves a privileged class and had identified themselves with the system of oppression. In Antrim and Down, Protestants, both Anglican and Presbyterian, rose against the landlords' armies and the British. In Mayo, poor peasants gathered to march inland to eventual defeat with the small French force that had landed at Killala. The year 1798 was a year of blood, a year of great confusion, a year in which 'the common name of Irishman' was disowned.

The insurrections were bloodily and brutally put down, and the Union was passed. But violence continued, and in 1803 Robert Emmet led a further, quickly suppressed, attempt at insurrection in Dublin. Emmet's elder brother was one of the 1798 United Irishmen who had suffered execution. Emmet himself suffered a traitor's death on a scaffold outside St. Catherine's church in Dublin. He, more than Tone, set the romantic pattern for the nationalism of the nineteenth century. His attempt to overthrow the British government in Ireland may have been, in the outcome, trivial (although it had been intelligently planned), but Emmet was the romantic hero *apar excellence*, fully in the mould of that Napoleonic era. His speech from the dock after conviction, his demeanour on the public scaffold, his expression of love and devotion to, not abstract principles, but his country, made him a model for balladeers and a saint of the burgeoning nineteenth-century religion of nationalism:

Hung, drawn and quartered, sure that was my sentence;
But soon I will show them, no coward am I;
My crime was the love of the land I was born in;
A hero I lived and a hero I'll die.

Bold Robert Emmet, the darlin' of Erin,
Bold Robert Emmet, that died with a smile;
Farewell, companions, both loyal and darin'
— I lay down my life for the Emerald Isle.

In the ballads of early nineteenth century Dublin, the heroes of nationalism rubbed shoulders happily enough with other folk-heroes, victims of hangmen, bailiffs, sheriffs, judges and the other hated lackeys of the law — with rapparees, highwaymen, rogues, and the ever popular perpetrators of *crimes passionels*. In the drawing rooms of the middle class, the songs of Emmet's friend Tom Moore, 'Ireland's national poet' as he was universally acknowledged to be in his time, offered a more sentimental and harmless version of nationalism, sighing over vanished glories and dead heroes and heroines. Moore's *Irish Melodies* translated, into the anodyne elegiac song of the Victorian drawing room, faint echoes of the outcry of the poor and the dispossessed. Faint though they were, these echoes were to acquire force and meaning.

Meantime the remote past was quarried for symbols for the nationalism that gathered force in resentment at Ireland's circumstances under the Union. Tara, for example, came to symbolize the imagined glory of ancient Ireland. Tara was the scene of an extraordinary occasion in 1843, when Daniel O'Connell was campaigning for the repeal of the Union. O'Connell, a lawyer of great capacity and a member of a native and Cathol'c landlord family that had survived, in Kerry, in spite of the repeated confiscations of Catholic land, had led the political movement that culminated in the Catholic Emancipation Act of 1829. This did away with almost all the penal laws that still remained on the statute book, and allowed O'Connell himself and other Roman Catholics, both British and Irish, to enter the Westminster parliament.

It was under his leadership that Irish people showed the talent for political ᴄrganization and the grasp of popular politics that have since marked them, both at home and abroad. The Irish in the nineteenth century played a large part in the introduction of democracy into the oligarchic British system, and have a fair claim — with due regard to that of Andrew Jackson in America — to priority in the introduction of mass democracy to the modern world. Contemporary accounts report that more than half a million people heard O'Connell speak on the hill of Tara in 1843. This may be an exaggeration, but there is no doubt that the 'Liberator', as O'Connell had come to be known, drew vast crowds to his meetings. As these meetings in that year were sometimes taking place in locations, like Tara, whose very names evoked nationalistic pride, the British government became extremely alarmed at the marshalling of such huge numbers of people. They banned a meeting at Clontarf on the

O' Connell monument, Glasnevin, Dublin

Dublin, after the Rising

The statue of James Larkin, O'Connell Street, Dublin

The statue of Edmund Burke by John Henry Foley, Trinity College, Dublin

Excavation of the Viking site at Wood Quay, Dublin

The new civic offices at Wood Quay, Dublin

outskirts of Dublin later in the year. To the people of 1843, Clontarf was the place where, in the battle of 1014, Brian Boru, high king of Ireland, had, once and for all, broken the power of the Danes and freed Ireland. The symbolism was plain. But O'Connell (although he was no pacifist) refused to call on force in the presentation of what he and his millions of followers saw as Ireland's case against England.

This campaign came to an unsuccessful end with the banning of the Clontarf meeting, but the strength and extent of the support O'Connell commanded showed that the Union of 1801 was a failure. It had failed to gain the assent of most Irish people. They wanted a separate Irish parliament and government. Through the second half of the nineteenth century the country remained all but ungovernable. There were many nationalist organizations and campaigns, including some that tried to promote further armed uprisings. The famine of the 1840s was seen by very many as a consequence, simply, of British rule. This interpretation was carried away by the hundreds of thousands who fled the stricken country and began the movement of emigration that was to bring millions of Irish to the New World.

O'Connell was a champion of the Irish Catholics. To them indeed he was 'the Liberator'. He was a liberal, in the early-nineteenth-century mould of, say, Montalambert, with more than a touch of Bentham. He campaigned for civil and human rights. He strongly opposed what he called the 'Orange hegemony' in Ireland. To the Irish Protestants he offered open arms; but it was plain that in Ireland after repeal of the union majority rule would prefail. This a large body of the Protestants would not have, and, especially in Ulster, they mounted effective opposition to his campaign. Long after his death, the unveiling of the sculptural monument to him at the south end of Sackville Street in Dublin provoked serious rioting a hundred miles away, in Belfast.

Meantime, others organised in the belief that the Union could not be broken by peaceful agitation and argument; that on this issue Britain would yield only to force. Young Ireland in 1848 and the Fenians in 1867 attempted uprisings, which were miserable fiascos, for lack of planning and coordination, for lack of preparation and means, and because Dublin Castle's informers kept up an adequate supply of intelligence to the authorities. But, in a sense, even the parliamentary and peaceful agitators relied upon the threat of force. The 'men of violence', as they are nowadays referred to in the British and Irish media of communication, always stood in the shadows behind O'Connell, and his successors as Irish leaders, Parnell and Redmond. O'Connell's language was violent and menacing: argument was backed by the menace of its alternative: force. What gave nationalist agitation in Ireland its cutting edge, as it were, in relation to England was the hint, or half-hint, that behind it lay the threat of the alternative tradition. Nor was this ambiguity to be confined to the nationalist side of the Irish argument. The supporters of the Union too, from the beginning, backed up parliamentary persuasion with the threat of violence. It was unionism indeed which brought the gun, permanently it would sometimes seem, into twentieth-century Irish politics.

And it was the physical force tradition that gave Dublin its most dramatic, destructive and metamorphic week, at Easter 1916. Four years earlier the Third Home Rule bill, to give Ireland its own parliament in Dublin, with very limited devolved powers, was introduced and passed the House of Commons at Westminster. The Lords could, and did, hold it up for two years. This gave the opponents of the bill time to organise, which they did, most effectively in Ulster. There a military force, the Ulster Volunteer Force, was established and proceeded to arm itself to resist the bill, threatening to call on German aid against Britain if necessary. In Dublin a counterpart body was founded, the Irish Volunteers, to support the implementation of Home Rule. The major political and constitutional crisis that ensued was overtaken and interrupted by the outbreak of the European war in August 1914.

Both the principal nationalist political leader, John Redmond, and the unionist leader, Carson, offered support to the British government in the war against Germany and Austria. The Home Rule bill became law in September, but was immediately suspended for the duration of hostilities in Europe. It was the leaders of a breakaway group of the Irish Volunteers, together with those of a small Marxist force, the Irish Citizen Army, who decided that Home Rule was a failure and that they should strike at British rule in Ireland while Britain was engaged in the war. Their plans for a countrywide rising went badly awry, but on Easter Monday 1916, they seized parts of central Dublin and held them through a week's heavy fighting against the British garrison troops in Ireland and reinforcements that were brought in by sea.

A decade of turmoil followed. The rising was suppressed and numbers of its leaders were executed by firing squad. But within a matter of months popular opinion began to move to the support of the 'physical force' as distinct from the parliamentary movement for Irish independence, and in 1918, immediately after the end of the Great War, the Irish electorate, in a general election, returned a great majority of members of 'Sinn Féin' — the republican party — who had undertaken not to take their seats in Westminster but to assemble in Dublin as the parliament of Ireland —Dáil Éireann. This they duly did (or those who were not in gaol did) at the beginning of 1919, and declared an Irish republic. The British attempt to suppress Dáil Éireann and the Irish Republic led to more than two years of guerrilla warfare, assassinations, government reprisals, including the burning of towns and villages, and, eventually, a truce. In the meantime, the Home Rule act of 1914 had been abandoned, and the British parliament passed the Government of Ireland Act, 1920, which partitioned Ireland, cutting off six of the Ulster counties from the rest. The rest, twenty-six counties, now known as the Irish Free State, became a Dominion of the British Empire, under the crown.

So Dublin became the capital of a dismembered Ireland, a capital whose first government functioned in a state of siege. For civil war followed the setting up of the Irish Free State, since the terms of the Anglo-Irish Treaty were rejected by a large section of the republicans, including many units of the Volunteers, or 'Irish Republican Army', as they had come to be known. Fighting was destructive in Dublin. The Four Courts, occupied by republican forces, were bombarded by the army of the Free State, causing the explosion of a store of munitions and the incidental destruction of the Public Record Office and a large part of its contents. Many of the buildings in O'Connell street that had not been destroyed in the 1916 fighting were destroyed now.

But by the mid 1920s, the Free State government had prevailed, and Dublin began slowly to take on a new character. The whole country had been transformed in the previous half-century as successive British governments had responded to Irish pressures by a series of enactments which amounted in sum to a social revolution. The Anglican church had been disestablished in Ireland. Then a series of acts of parliament had transferred a large part of the land from the Ascendancy landlords to the tenants. The educational system had been expanded and, in part, transformed. And other institutional and administrative changes had been made. And then Dominion status had been achieved as the result of several years of fighting. In short, by the 1920s, ordinary Irish people, mostly Catholics, had taken over the control of most of Ireland.

Dublin was now the centre of what turned out to be a very centralised economy and policy. The city expanded its population, largely through migration from the country at large. Before independence it had been a city of slums, in which about a third of its inhabitants lived. Slum clearance now began and proceeded steadily. New housing estates expanded the city physically. By the end of the Second World War, in which Ireland was neutral, Dublin was approaching twice its population of the beginning of the century, although a policy of economic self-sufficiency and import-substition had kept Ireland conservative and relatively stagnant.

Then, about ten years after the war, new dramatic changes began, in association with the development of new economic policies which opened the former Free State (now a Republic) to foreign investment and trade. The changes became more marked after Ireland's entry into the E.E.C. in 1973 — although this more or less coincided with the onset of economic crisis in the West at large. By the mid 1980s, Dublin's population had doubled again (it is now over a million people) and the appearance of the city was rapidly changing. The general crisis was affecting Ireland, and particularly Dublin, severely, as unemployment, crime and violence increased, in line with most of the large cities of the western world.

6
LITERATURE

Before it became the capital of the Irish Free State, Dublin was the centre of a remarkable literary revival. From the background of its nineteenth-century suburbs and inner city streets and squares; from its concert halls and cultural societies and political clubs; from the tensions, anxieties, hostilities, aspirations and ideals generated by the underlying conflicts of Irish life under the Union, Dublin produced a succession of writers in English who were to make a blazon on modern literature in the language: Wilde, Moore, Shaw, Yeats, Synge, Joyce, O'Casey and many more.

The background of this emergence is more complicated than it may seem at first sight. Anglo-Ireland already had a history replete with major writers in English, including Swift, Sheridan, Goldsmith and Burke. The people dominant in their world laid out handsome estates, built elegant houses, and created spacious and nobly designed towns and cities. They attended the theatre and applauded concerts of European music. Their culture was by no means wholly a verbal one, even if its flourishing was comparatively late (Ireland was not at peace until the beginning of the eighteenth century) and even if some of the conventional arts of the time, such as painting, were still more tardy in their development.

But there was another Ireland, that of the majority of the people. In the later Middle Ages, a hybrid culture flourished in Ireland, drawing, through the aristocrats and gentry descended from the Norman settlers of the twelfth and thirteenth centuries, and through those descended from the native Irish rulers of earlier times, on the traditions in literature, architecture, sculpture, painting and music of Ireland, England and France. But that Gaelic-speaking culture had been broken down and ultimately pulverised in a whole series of conflicts and onslaughts. The many wars and revolutions of the sixteenth and seventeenth centuries dispossessed and exiled its nobility and gentry, dispersed its schools of law, medicine and literature, degraded its language, persecuted its faith, destroyed its economy and customs, and reduced vast numbers of its people to pauperdom.

The poorer half (and they were very poor indeed) of the population of nineteenth-century Ireland were virtually without material possessions. The peasants of nineteenth-century Ireland, mostly, lacked the distinctive and colourful costumes, crafts and customs that distinguished peasant populations elsewhere in Europe. They had nothing to practice craft on. Medieval Ireland, a dairying country, had a great variety of cheeses and other milk products. Now there were none. And this is only one example of many to illustrate the breakdown in continuity of material culture and the depth of the traumas through which Irish society had passed.

This placed great emphasis on words and, to some extent, on music produced with very simple means including, notably, the human voice. Irish culture became intensely verbal. It had always been so, even when there was rich variety and high achievement in material art and crafts as well. It is plain from the very qualities of some early Irish literature that what was highly appreciated was wit: the elegant, spare, intelligent, subtle and revelatory use of words. The thought that leaps several stages of reasoning and, in the process, challenges itself and overcomes the challenge: that was the use of words. This quality to some extent survived the harrowing and drastic change of language, from Irish to English, that was happening throughout modern times. At least it survived it into the first one or two generations of English speakers. But it was the Irish speakers, still very numerous in the nineteenth century, who inherited the great wealth and variety of oral tradition from the ages of Gaelic dominance.

So, if the literary culture of late-eighteenth-century colonial Ireland, writing in English, derived most of its qualities from the native traditions of the English language, the Anglo-Irish writers of the late nineteenth century had a culture enhanced, to greater or less degree, by the influence of the oral tradition of Irish. A century or more of antiquarian activity had gradually opened up knowledge of the civilization of early Ireland and had brought about a profoundly changed perception of the past that lay behind the impoverished and often destitute peasants of the west. The view, commonly held among the Ascendancy of the eighteenth century, that the light of European civilization had first been brought to Ireland by Henry II and his barons in the twelfth century, could no longer be sustained, and there was now a romantic impulse to assert Irish nationality by going to the well-springs of Celtic culture. As the Anglo-Irish lost their grip on both economic and political power, largely through the actions of British governments, they tried to strengthen the Irish links of their hyphenated ambivalence.

Ireland had an extensive oral literature and tradition before the establishment of Christianity in the country made writing common. Laws, genealogies, histories, myth and tales were transmitted by a learned caste of experts who placed great emphasis in their prolonged training on the cultivation of memory. Poets were seers, with semi-divine powers: the recital of verses was little removed from the utterance of oracles or spells.

At a very early date some of the learned class became acquainted with the scripts of the Continent. A rune-like cipher was developed, based on the Roman alphabet, in which groups of strokes or notches represent the letters. This was used for brief epigraphic inscriptions and perhaps for a few other purposes. The epigraphs are found on the upright edges of squared pillar stones, but it would appear from references in the literature that the most common medium for ogham writing may have been wood —sticks notched and scored with brief messages. Professor James Carney, of the Dublin Institute of Advanced Studies, has demonstrated that the origin of the ogham cipher may be a good deal earlier than used to be thought, and that its place of origin was probably in Continental Europe, most likely Roman Gaul.

It has long been conventional to associate the beginnings of literacy with the beginnings of Christianity in Ireland, and to date both to about the fifth century. But there certainly were Christians in Ireland before then, and it seems very likely that there were also people in Ireland acquainted with writing much earlier than the fifth century. Since the earliest Irish literary tradition, like that of the Continental Celts, was oral, the absence of early writings may be a reflection not merely of ignorance but also of an opposition to the writing down of lore which people were expected to memorize.

Christianity however required the existence of books, and once the new religion was spread in Ireland we find that the making and decorating of books became outstanding features of Irish culture. The book, along with the bell and the crosier, is one of the conventional symbols used to identify ecclesiastics in early Irish art, and the interest of the Irish in books was one of the characteristics for which they were noted abroad. We have no evidence at all that any form of painting was practised in pre-Christian Ireland, but once psalters and Gospel-books had to be provided, we find that the scribes and craftsmen soon developed a style and technique for ornamenting their manuscripts with rich and elaborate paintings, using pigments some of which must have been imported. The word was honoured.

This development took place at a time when significant changes were taking place in written materials. The ancient Greco-Roman world had depended largely on supplies of papyrus from Egypt for the making of written records. This was a comparatively fragile and perishable material, but it was also comparatively cheap. It was usually manufactured in long scrolls, which could be kept in tubular containers, and this was the common form of early books. Changes in economic and trading patterns in the post-Roman period, including the major changes brought about by the Muslim conquest of North Africa, caused a diminution in the supplies of papyrus reaching northern Europe and the West. Our earliest surviving manuscripts from Ireland are all on a quite different material, vellum, that is, specially prepared calf-skin, and they are in codex form; in other words they are bound with leaves in the general fashion to which we are accustomed in present-day books. Vellum, properly prepared and reasonably well looked after, will last almost indefinitely.

The language of the early books is Latin, but we know that the Latin alphabet had already been adapted to serve the purposes of Irish by the time of the oldest books that still survive (about the end of the sixth century). The ogham inscriptions, which are in Irish, are based on a Latin alphabet. They are of course brief and usually of a funerary or memorial character. A system of notches and strokes, such as ogham is, is suitable for short inscriptions on sticks or wooden posts, or on the edge of a rough stone pillar, but is far too cumbersome for general use in books. The writing in the books therefore is in no sense a development from or an 'improvement' on ogham writing, but something with quite a different purpose. Instead the ogham inscriptions may tell us about the very early borrowings of the Latin alphabet which have not survived in the form of straightforward writing. In part at least this alphabet was associated in Ireland with the Christian mission. In seventh-century accounts of St. Patrick's legend, for example, we find stories which tell how he wrote alphabets for his converts, or left alphabets with them when he moved on. And in Kilmalkedar on the Dingle peninsula in Co. Kerry, there is an early cross-inscribed pillar which has an alphabet incised, rather clumsily, down one face.

The first Irishman whose mind is open to us, through a sufficient written record is the monk Columbanus, who went in his middle age at the end of the sixth century from the monastery of Bangor (Co. Down) to Gaul, and founded monasteries there and in northern Italy. Of his writings there now remain a few letters, poems and hymns, and instructions and homilies for his monastic community. In him we meet a headstrong, proud and dedicated man, wholly committed to his faith, securely confident (in the context of the ecclesiastical controversies of his time) in the soundness of his Irish education and training. His Latin is lively, his style somewhat mannered and given to word-play, his reading, as shown by the citation of a variety of works, quite wide, his enjoyment of the pagan Latin classics unhampered by his piety. Columbanus is not a major writer, but in him there steps out of the darkness of prehistory a recognisable Irishman, bearing the stamp of the culture that formed him.

The Irish soon developed their own, generally less stylish, variant of late Latin. One school developed an ornate euphuistic style, designed, it would seem, to show off their knowledge of obscure words and expressions. An output of saints' lives began in the seventh century, but the interest of the hagrography is not literary. Whatever small merit the earliest saints' lives had, many of the later ones had none. There were some passable poets in Latin, such as Sedulius Scottus, and writers of expository prose, such as Eriugena, the philosopher.

But writing in Latin is quite overshadowed by writing in Irish. Once an orthography had been devised for this, the oral learning, in its various branches, came to be written down. The heroic literature includes many epic tales of kings and queens, gods and goddesses, heroes and warriors. Irish epic is in prose, with occasional (often obscure) passages in verse. The prose is spare, wasting no words, but conveying an atmosphere and moving the narrative along. In the older epic the world depicted is such that, as we have seen, the Celtic scholar Kenneth Jackson could describe it as 'a window on the Iron Age'. It depicts a society remarkably similar to that described centuries earlier by Greek and Roman writers in accounts of the Continental Celts before the Roman conquests. Much of the earliest narrative concerns itself with the doings of a king of Emhain Mhacha —the royal centre of the Ulaid, near present-day Armagh — and his warriors and with warfare on the borders of Ulster. The chief saga of this group, *Táin Bó Cuailgne* (the 'cattle-raid of Cuailgne'), was once recited and known in every part of Ireland.

Other sagas were concerned with the shadowy kings of the beginning of the historical period, with mythological characters and heroes, and with love-tales, adventures and voyages. A coherent view of the world emerges, a view appropriate to a society just emerging from a Celtic tribal organisation to one of chiefdoms which would in due course develop into states. Life and death are accepted unsentimentally, as in the epic of other literatures; this world is interpenetrated by an Otherworld in which divine and semi-divine beings have their place; there is a very clear concept of Ireland as a cultural, or at times a cosmic, entity, the bounding sea round the island is given an almost mystic significance; and there is a sharp distinction between the nobles, whose hierarchies form the societies in which action takes place, and people of low degree, who hardly figure in the stories at all.

Prose writers in due course produced works in Irish dealing with a range of other subjects, including law, genealogy, history, chronology and other subjects for description and exposition. A special category was the 'History of Places', a topic which has commanded much interest in Ireland through all the centuries since then. One of the commonest types of ballad or ditty popular in rural Ireland today consists largely of placenames in songs of praise, nostalgia or sentimentality about some part of the country — usually, nowadays, a county.

It is plain that in pagan Ireland the poet, like the king, was a sacred figure having special powers of communication with the Otherworld. The poet and the druid belonged to the same category of protected and privileged persons. With the coming of Christianity, the clerics, more or less, came to occupy the same status and privileged position as their predecessors the druids. There is a pseudo-historical tale which tells how one of the greatest of the early monastic leaders, Columba (Columcille) in the sixth century at an assembly in the north of Ireland saved the poets of Ireland from banishment. Their order, it was said, had become so greedy and arrogant that it had been decided to do away with them, but the saint, himself trained as a poet, pleaded eloquently on their behalf and secured a reprieve. So the poets went on exercising their mysterious powers, patronised and protected by kings and nobles who maintained them and gave them gifts in return for praise poems, and who dreaded the satire which could be provoked by the mean or the niggardly, or those who otherwise offended the poets. Satire, it was said, could cause blisters and other physical blemishes in those against whom it was directed. Faint traces of the centuries-long belief in the power of the poet still also linger in present-day Ireland, at least among the poets.

It would seem that in prehistoric, pagan, times (to judge from episodes in the sagas) poets and seers were often women. In the earliest literature, women function as autonomous, often powerful beings. Although the society of early historic Ireland was to be, like other Indo-European societies, male-dominated, it retained many traces — and more than traces — of an earlier and different order, on which, presumably, the *Feni* or *Scotti* had imposed a system like that of the Continental Celts. The schools of poetry were male, but women patronised poetry and poets; throughout the long history of Gaelic literature there were from time to time to be notable women poets; and in the whole area of love-literature women were the active characters, as protagonists and often as writers.

Irish poetry was syllabic, not stressed, and the metres were extremely complex and difficult, with elaborate rules of rhyme, half-rhyme, assonance, the matching of certain categories of consonants with one another, and so on. Meaning aside, the composing of a poem was like the composing of a fugue. But of course meaning had to go in too. This was a highly professional art which required long training. Like other arts and crafts it was generally an hereditary trade.

While the formal or set-piece poems dazzle more by their technical accomplishment than by their truth of feeling and thought, the great variety of work produced in the centuries from the sixth to the twelfth includes a wealth of brilliant and piercing lyric verse, often brief quatrains, exquisitely sparing of language. A striking feature of the work is that so much of it is nature-poetry, sharply descriptive and evocative, like the Japanese *haiku*. Kenneth Jackson wrote that this early literature 'did not belong at all to the common culture of western Europe', and Seamus Heaney wrote of it:

'And it is this surge towards praise — this sudden apprehension of the world as light, as illumination — this is what remains central to our first nature poetry and this makes it a unique inheritance.'

But the nature poetry also has a religious significance. The early Christians struggled against the widespread belief in the autonomous power of nature's forces: the sun, the wind, the sky, the sea. Some of the Continental Celts told Alexander the Great that the only thing they feared on earth was that the sky might fall upon them. The pagan Irish swore their most solemn oaths by the sky, the wind and the sun. Christianity taught that God had power over all these forces — in St. Patrick's meagre writings this is one of the sermon-themes that comes across most clearly — and the hermits and monks who wrote many of these poems were celebrating not just nature's beauty, sensual immediacy and revelation of life, but that it was all in God's hand:

Here's a song —
stags give tongue
winter snows
summer goes

High cold blow
sun is low
brief his day
seas give spray

Fern clumps redden
shapes are hidden
wildgeese raise
wonted cries.

Cold now girds
wings of birds
icy time —
that's my rhyme.

That (here given in Flann O'Brien's translation) is one of many.

The scribes provided Gospel-books and psalters for the increasingly numerous churches in the sixth and seventh centuries. Then they began copying a growing variety of texts. Tastes changed from century to century. The sharpness of earlier work gives way to more ornate styles. Epic was replaced by romantic tales, including the large cycle of medieval stories and verse relating to the *Fianna*, bands of warrior-hunters who had adventures throughout Ireland in a never-never time of the past. One of the great romantic stories in this cycle, *The Pursuit of Diarmait and Grainne*, with its elegiac overtones, may be compared with the bleak epic tale, *The Sorrowful Tale of the Sons of Uisneach* (the story of Deirdre) from the much earlier Ulster cycle.

But the principal story of the old cycle was *Táin Bo Cuailgne*, often referred to simply as 'the *Táin*' (although there are other *Tána* in the storytelling). The earliest manuscripts containing this story date from the twelfth century, but the one which was copied in Clonmacnoise early in that century, *Lebor na hUidre* (the 'book of the dun cow') is written in the Irish of a much earlier date. In the *Book of Leinster*, copied in the second half of the twelfth century there is a later and more ornate version of the tale.

The *Táin* is a prose epic, with passages of verse, in which it conforms to the general pattern of the early Irish sagas. It draws on the common body of material of the Ulster cycle to compose a narrative, quite intricately interwoven even in the imperfect renderings that have come down to us, concerned with ancient warfare between the *Ulaid* and invaders of their province from other parts of Ireland. The saga is an elaboration, almost certainly, of a primitive mythological tale concerning conflict between two divine bulls. But anthropomorphic goddesses and gods entered the picture, and then were euhemerised into human queens, kings and heroes.

The classic opening of the saga is the 'pillow-talk' of Medb, queen of Connacht, and her husband Ailill as they recline in bed and begin to enumerate their respective possessions. These prove to be exactly equal except that among his herds Ailill has a magnificent bull, which Medb can't match. But there does exist such a bull, in south-east Ulster, among the mountains of the Cooley peninsula in what is now Co. Louth (*Cuailgne*). The owner of the bull refuses to part with it on terms Medb offers, and she decides to take it by force. She musters armies, not only those of Connacht, but contingents drawn from all over Ireland. The warriors of the Ulaid must suffer the pains of childbirth for a number of days before they can come to defend their endangered frontier. This is because of a curse, the subject of another story in the cycle, imposed on them by an Otherworld woman whom they had compelled to run a race at the end of which, victorious, she had died giving birth to twins. But the Ulaid have a great champion, Cuchulainn, who is immune because he is not by origin an Ulsterman. He defends the pass, meeting the chief warriors of Ireland in a series of single combats. This is the outline of the story which is told with many asides and by-tales, including narratives of Cuchulainn's youth and apprenticeship to the warrior's trade.

The tradition, embodied in versions of the *Táin* itself, was that the *Táin* had been 'lost' for a while; that none of the poets of Ireland could remember the great epic, and that it was found only after search and divination. It may be that for a time the story, like other tales from the pagan past, was frowned on in the monasteries which were the main means of transmission of this literature. But in due course the native literary and scholarly tradition prevailed over the Romanising prejudices that arrived with Christianity, and the church came to terms with the poets.

The poetic schools continued to function throughout the Middle Ages and a little while beyond. Norman settlers, and after them English and Scottish landlords, continued to patronise the Gaelic poets — right down to the early nineteenth century. New varieties of work were produced in Ireland until the early modern period, but the whole system, of education, training, patronage and communication, on which the literature depended was destroyed by war, confiscation, and the anglicization of the ruling orders of society. By the later seventeenth century the high culture of Gaelic literature had broken down. There now ensued the development of a popular literature, with new kinds of verse — stressed rather than syllabic, with much less complex verbal and sound structures. This produced, mainly in the eighteenth and early nineteenth centuries, a new flowering, of quite a different kind. There is a wealth of love poetry, religious poetry, political poetry, nature poetry, produced by poor poets whose patronage was doled out to them in the kitchens of the landlords' houses and whose schools were periodical meetings with their fellows in taverns. The influence of English and Continental literature gave rise to some new forms, as in the long masterpiece, *The Midnight Court*, written in Co. Clare in 1780 by Brian Merriman.

By the middle of the nineteenth century this tradition too was all but dead. But the first stirrings of the language revival movement began to open up the knowledge of this literature, however imperfectly, to a wider world. (A hundred years earlier Macpherson's *Ossian* had introduced European culture to its existence.) And in the twentieth century, in the dwindling Irish-speaking areas, yet another renaissance in Irish writing took place, largely among writers who, although living in the west of Ireland, were well acquainted with European literature and could address a sophisticated if small audience.

The later stages of the development of Gaelic literature were much affected by the influence of literature in other languages, notably French and English. French was widely spoken by the nobility and gentry of Norman origin in the twelfth, thirteenth and fourteenth centuries, and Seán O Tuama in a fine study *An Grá in Amhrán na nDaoine* (Love in Folk Song) has shown how themes from *amour courtois* and other Continental modes passed from the great houses to the people and were transformed into folk-poetry and folksong.

There is a long *chanson* of the early thirteenth century, 'The Song of Dermot and the Earl', in Norman French, which is one of the chief sources for the events of the Cambro-Norman invasion of the twelfth century. Another Norman-French poem of half a century or more later, *Rithmus facture Ville de Rosse*, describes the building of the walls of New Ross (Co. Wexford) and is colourful in its account of the different classes of people then inhabiting the town.

But gradually English made headway against French, becoming in time the language of the English-occupied towns. In the countryside, Irish made headway against both French and English, and some of the great Hiberno-Norman lords of the Middle Ages were themselves accomplished poets in Irish. But the colony in Ireland in due course began to produce its own literature in English. Kildare, Kilkenny and Dublin were among the centres where religious and secular verse and some prose were written. The religious work is frequently fairly gloomy in character:

> This world's love is gone away
> As dew on grass in summer's day,
> Few there be, well-a-way,
> That love God His lore,

as Friar Michael of Kildare sums it up in a few lines from a long poem of the late thirteenth century. Some of the secular verse is no less gloomy, and much of it leaves the impression that the English colony in medieval Ireland was not a very cheerful one:

> Hate and wrath there is full rife,
> And true love is full thin,
> Men that be in highest life
> Most charged be with sin.

But some, notably satirical work like *The Land of Cockaygne*, is much more lively.

The English colony was in decline after the numerous disasters (including the Black Death) of the fourteenth century, and its literature, such as it was, faded in significance and is all but forgotten — although there have been occasional borrowings, by Yeats and others in modern times.

The English conquest of Ireland in the course of the sixteenth century, and the establishment of the new 'Ascendancy' order as a result of the British revolutionary upheavals of the seventeenth century and the consequent war and confiscations in Ireland, produced a new cultural landscape. When an exhausted peace came, by the beginning of the eighteenth century, the Gaelic social order had been extirpated, the descendants and inheritors of the tradition of the medieval English colony had largely (as Roman Catholics) been dispossessed or exiled, and a new Protestant colony, established on large estates and building country houses throughout the land, had Dublin as its centre and Trinity College as its intellectual focus. By the end of the eighteenth century, especially with the foundation of the Royal Irish Academy in 1785, a new intellectual centre (although still closely connected with Trinity) was to be established in Dublin, with great importance for the direction of minds to the country's ancient inheritance.

In the meantime, the eighteenth century, if peaceful enough almost to its close, was a time of great underlying strain and tension as a dominant people and a (greatly more numerous) subject people shared the island very unevenly, and looked at it with very different eyes.

Much of what was written at that time, whether in English or in Irish, whether in verse or in prose, whether fiction or philosophy, is coloured by the quite unusual, if not unique, situation of the different orders in society, who were sharply distinguished in law by the series of legal enactments against 'popery' that placed the large majority of the population under a penal regime. But there was not simply a dichotomy between oppressors and oppressed, which is common enough in the world. The oppressed cherished the memory of their own distinctive civilization, with its own social and cultural rules. They didn't merely resent the new ruling order: they despised it, as upstart, heretical, uncouth and ignorant of the true ordering of life. While the ruling order in turn despised the conquered people for their poverty, for their defeat, for their ignorance of true civilization, for their superstitious religion, and, in time, for the cunning which the dispossessed developed as a weapon in their struggle for survival. Among the Ascendancy it was, on the whole, the writers whose open minds and eyes led them to perceive something of the reality of this contrast. Almost everything that has endured of the writings of eighteenth-century Irishmen has reference to politics, or at least shows awareness of an almost cosmic injustice.

Swift, Irish by domicile, expressed in the plainest of prose (worthy of the writers who had trodden the same earth a thousand years before his time) his magnificent discontent at being imprisoned in corruption, of the flesh, of an unredeemed society. But he did this on the ground of Dublin, and with the particularity of Irish misery in his mind. And for the poor of Dublin he was a friend. Burke was to move from a youthful rage at the same particularities to a mature and sustained endeavour, justifying men's ways to God, that was to earn him his place as the mentor of modern conservatism (and the comfort, in intellectual distress, of liberals). Berkeley, Goldsmith, and the orators like Flood, Grattan and Curran, spoke from the same knowledge that there was some terrible flaw in their universe, and they were in time to colour the minds of men and women who moved from words to actions.

The writers of the earlier nineteenth century, on the whole, are not nowadays as well regarded as some of them were in their time or as some of the eighteenth-century writers still are. But the underlying questions, with their political edge, persisted. Tom Moore, once rated with Byron and Burns, no longer enjoys that esteem, perhaps because of the failure of nerve that marked his literary as well as his political intentions, although he tried bravely enough according to his means.

But later in the century the strange soil of Irish society produced a new crop of literary fruit. Oscar Wilde's father was a man of many and varied talents, virtues and vices. His mother was a passionately romantic nationalist versifier. The contradiction and confusion of Ireland under the Union was his background, and the closed-circle disputatiousness of Dublin. From this he brought a honed wit, a deep understanding of the volcanos under all our feet, and a tenacious capacity to make of honour, in a corrupt world, the stuff of literature. Wilde's work is brave, true and witty, and it consistently challenges the Panglossian lie that, of necessity, sustains all imperial systems. In this he was joined by another keen mind (although perhaps not so deep) from a different Dublin background: that of Shaw.

And then, in the 1890s, politics, revolutionary social change, nationalism, the confrontation of a traditional society by the modern world, and the effects of the achievement of theoretical political equality by Catholics; all these produced in their coming together political, social and literary upheaval.

The Ascendancy for a century and a half had provided (largely from its fringes) leadership for those who opposed as well as for those who supported the Glorious Revolution and the Union. It now produced its last leaders, not in politics but in literature, for the Catholic as well as the Protestant people of Ireland. Yeats and Synge followed, to some degree, a pattern established in the previous generation, but by now the recovery of the Gaelic past was having a very great effect in the worlds of literature and politics. Douglas Hyde, another Anglo-Irishman, had acquired a command of Irish and had been publishing the songs of the people of Connacht. The Gaelic League was founded in 1893 and Hyde, as its president, agitated to turn back the tide of Anglicization. Yeats, more widely, was to take up arms (as Cuchulainn in the Ulster saga did against the sea) against the 'filthy modern tide'. While Synge rediscovered the patterns of Celtic myth, and set the themes of the goddesses and the gods among the islanders and fishing people of the west, Yeats, with his powerfully creative mind, attempted, almost single-handed, to create an alternative world to the shoddy commercial world that late-nineteenth-century imperialism made. He was not without success, for a while.

But leadership, in literature as in politics, was shifting from the Anglo-Irish. James Joyce and Michael Collins mark a different kind of resurgence. But there is, again, a continuity. They too attempted to raise the banner of honour against corruption. Collins attempted it in spite of the close contact with evil that terrorism or guerrilla war involves. Joyce attempted it in the form of 'silence, exile and cunning'.

Portrait of James Joyce in Davy Byrne's Pub, Dublin

The Statue of George Bernard Shaw at the National Gallery, Dublin

Samuel Beckett

Edward Maguire's portrait of Seamus Heaney, Ulster Museum, Belfast

Again, with Joyce, bravery, truth and wit produce a literature.

And, north and south of the Border, Ireland has continued to be guided by the imagination of writers. Between the wars, Seán O Faoláin, Frank O'Connor and some others attempted to leaven the spirit of an Ireland exhausted and insecure after the long effort to find a way to the future different from England's. Since the Second World War, as a great social, political, moral and economic crisis developed throughout the island, a new literature has emerged, but one which is in many ways more inward-looking than the literature of the turn of the century. The contradictions and tensions of Irish society persist, and Irish writing continues to have a sharp political edge.

Ireland, in spite of the great economic depression of the mid 1980s, with its consequent effects on society and morale, is a country with a population that reads. Book sales, per capita, are high. In large shopping centres bookshops thrive, selling a great range of books concerned, one way and another, with Ireland, or with the problems of the world today. People have lost trust in politicians but appear to retain it in writers, especially imaginative writers. The poets, in particular, retain something of an ancient power, and Heaney, Kinsella, Montague, Longley, Simmons, Ó Ríordáin, Ó Direáin, Cronin, Ní Chuilleanáin, Ní Dhomhnaill and many more speak directly to young Ireland.

7

THE PROVINCES

The modern Irish word for 'province' is *cúige*. It derives from an old word meaning 'fifth'. The *cúige* in pre-Norman Ireland was a state, and each of the states embraced a number of smaller units. Among the states themselves there came to be a competition for hegemony and for the elevation of the ruler of one of them to high-kingship of all Ireland.

In spite of the name, at no time in the full historic period were there exactly five provinces. The number changed as some states were subdivided or amalgamated. So the term 'fifth' may refer to some late prehistoric arrangement, or, more likely, to an idealized picture of the divisions of Ireland. But the very idea of reckoning such division shows that there was something to divide. It indicates that, going back before the beginnings of history, there was a concept of Ireland as an entity or unity (although not a political one).

This is a very important concept, so deeply embedded in Irish consciousness as to have an undiminished significance down to the present day.

The idealized picture was probably one of a simple fivefold mandala-type division: north, south, east, west and centre: Ulster, Munster, Leinster and Connacht, in modern terminology, with a central kingdom. The central kingdom existed in early historic times and was called *Mide*, which means 'middle'.

The four quarters were given their attributes in early Irish cosmology. To abbreviate slightly an old text: the north was the place of battles, hardihood, rough places, strife, haughtiness, unprofitableness, pride, hardness; the south was the place of music, waterfalls, fairs, knowledge, subtlety, musicianship, melody, honour, chess-playing, poetical art; the east was the place of prosperity, supplies, beehives, householders, nobles, splendour, abundance, treasure, satin, serge, silk cloths, hospitality; the west was the place of learning, foundations, teaching, judgment, chronicles, counsels, stories, histories, science. In other words: Ulster for war; Munster for art; Leinster for wealth; Connacht for learning.

Leaving such fancies aside, we have in modern Ireland four, not five provinces. They have no political significance. There are no social, administrative or other authorities that correspond to the provinces, which function as entities only in sport. Yet most people feel that, however vaguely, the provinces have each an identity.

People nowadays will most readily see Ulster as the province with a distinct character. Six of its nine counties, after all, are politically separate from the rest of Ireland and are still part of the United Kingdom. Those who favour that Union often argue that from the beginning of history Ulster had a distinctive character. This is true; but, then, so had Munster, Leinster and Connacht.

The physical features of the old province of Ulster, however, give it one particular attribute of its own. The province is bounded on three sides by the sea and on the fourth, the south, by a swarm of low hump-back drumlin hills (deposited by the glaciation) with narrow rushy valleys between them, and by the winding waters of Erne, plaiting its divided streams round a myriad of islets and small spreading lakes. Hills rim the province, as they do the island of Ireland.

Ulster is a miniature Ireland. Through its lowland interior the river Bann flows northward, as the Shannon flows southward on the larger scale. And, just as the Shannon spreads out on its slow course into the lakes Allen, Ree and Derg, so the Bann in mid-course widens to form the broad Lough Neagh. There is a contrast, human and otherwise, between the country west of the Bann and the country to the east, just as there is a larger distinction made by the Shannon. But Ulster has sufficient regional unity. Across that unity the current Border winds erratically, dividing like from like.

A further parallel: Ulster, like Ireland as a whole, has had down the ages an intimate and often sad relationship with Britain. But, again, in its own way. A flight from Dublin to Glasgow or Edinburgh on a clear day brings home, more clearly than any map, the fact that the British and Irish live in an archipelago of large and small islands. The Irish Sea viewed from an aircraft flying north along the east coast at a low altitude assumes its character as an inland sea, rather than the oceanic divide it may appear to be when viewed from beach level.

Islands appear: first the Isle of Man; then — as the aircraft turns eastward at Larne — Arran, Bute, the Inner Hebrides, receding northward into a hazy distance. Crossing, in a couple of minutes, the North Channel, with this pattern of islands extending away on the left, one is hardly conscious of flying from one country to another. Nor does the L-shaped island of Rathlin, off the Antrim coast, seem much more appropriate to the Irish mainland than to the Mull of Kintyre, or the islands off the Clyde mouth.

This shading of Scotland into Ireland and Ireland into Scotland represents the history as well as the geography of the island-studded narrows at the northern entrance to the Irish Sea. Down the centuries people have moved freely to and fro among the islands and mainlands, bringing with them their customs, beliefs and ways of doing things. In very recent times, geologically speaking, the North Channel was not there at all, and Antrim was connected by land with Scotland.

The first, Mesolithic, settlers of Ireland probably came this way. The province of the builders of the court tombs in the megalithic age spanned the Channel. At the beginning of history the Antrim kingdom of Dál Riada was already established, and expanding, in Scotland, and its people, the 'Scots' (Irish) were to give north Britain its name, as well as the Gaelic language which was once spoken throughout the Highlands beyond. This colonising movement was soon followed by a Christian, monastic, colonisation. The movement to and fro continued through the Middle Ages. The heavily equipped mercenary troops with whom the Irish began to turn back the tide of Norman advance and conquest were Scots, or men of mixed Scots-Norse background — the Gallowgasses. And when James VI of Scotland succeeded Elizabeth I on the English throne and became James I of England, his Scottish subjects came crowding across the narrow sea-channel to settle in the north of Ireland, reversing the settlement of centuries before.

They came in greatest numbers to Antrim and north Down, but also settled fairly densely as far west as Donegal. They changed the pattern of life in the north very considerably, not least in that they were mostly Protestants of Calvinist persuasion. The government-organised Plantation of six confiscated Ulster counties in the early seventeenth century (Donegal, Derry, Tyrone, Fermanagh, Armagh and Cavan) brought in further settlement, of both Scots and English. And right down to the most recent times the orientation of the north coast of Ireland has shown in, for example, the annual movement of migrant workers to the potato-fields of Scotland, or the annual arrival, in the earlier part of this century, of Scottish herring-gutters to deal with the catch on the shore of Lough Swilly. To many people in Donegal, Glasgow has been more of a metropolis than Dublin, and far less distant in the real terms of human relations and direct acquaintance.

Ulster was the last part of Ireland to be brought fully under English rule, after the end of the sixteenth-century wars of conquest. Enniskillen, on the Erne, that stream which is more lake than river, was the frontier of Maguire's country, where, little influenced by the Normans, Gaelic civilization lived on until the end of the Middle Ages. On the other hand, in this countryside the Plantation of Ulster left an enduring imprint in towns and fortified bawns, tidy farms and a sturdy people. The town itself is a planter's foundation, established in 1612 by Captain William Cole, but it is at the strategic crossing of the river, between the upper lake and the lower, which was earlier occupied by a fifteenth-century fortified stronghold of the Maguires. Later, that tower house, enlarged in the sixteenth century, and with further additions still, was to become part of the complex of buildings which were the home of the Royal Inniskilling Fusiliers and the Royal Inniskilling Dragoons.

One of the distinctive features of eastern Ulster is that the region had an economic history quite unlike the rest of Ireland. It began with the linen industry, which for a long time was not urban but rural. Flax is a crop attested from very early times in Ireland, and linen has been made for centuries. There were many skilled weavers in the seventeenth-century migration from Britain to Ulster, and there was also a sponsored settlement of skilled Huguenot workers, refugees from religious persecution in France. The lifting of the British tax on the import of Irish plain linens in 1696, together with a restriction on Irish wool, gave a stimulus to the linen manufacturer.

The flax was grown in Ireland and was spun by women and woven by men in cottage homes, concentrated chiefly in the north. A Linen Board was established with government help in 1711 to regulate the trade, in which Dublin merchants, supplying the finance, played an important part. Most of the cloth was sold in Dublin before being re-sold in London. Linen-weaving, initially in the eighteenth century, brought considerable prosperity to the districts in which it was practised. An account from the 1750s says that '. . . from Monaghan quite to Carrickfergus, which is about fifty miles, is the very picture of industry, nor did I ever see in England or Ireland a finer cultivated country. The whole road for the space of fifty miles is, as it were, one continued village of neat cottages, for I believe in the whole space you are never two hundred yards distance from a pretty cabin, and what adds to the beauty is every cabin has a little orchard belonging to it, and spinning or weaving or some such branch of manufacture is going on in every house.'

County Armagh in the late eighteenth century had the highest density of population in rural Ireland, and it was precisely there, with pressure of population growth forcing keen competition for a livelihood, that serious Catholic-Protestant conflict began. It was affrays between gangs of Catholic 'Defenders' and Protestant 'Peep-o'-day-boys' that led to the foundation of the Orange order in 1795, the Protestant religious organisation that at the present day most colourfully expresses support for the Union.

That support is at its strongest east of the Bann, where Protestants are in a large majority of the population. The centre of this region is Belfast. No city in Ireland is more delightfully situated. It climbs up steep mountain slopes from its splendid Lough. The view from the hills to the sea over houses, spires, smoking chimneys and dockyard cranes and gantries gives an impression of busy space. On a bright day it also gives an impression of cleanliness and sparkle. Notoriously, a closer approach to the streets below the mountain leaves quite a different impression. The armoured cars and wary patrolling soldiers and police quickly dispel the sense of peacefulness, as does the violence of the slogans scrawled on dead walls. The rubble, charred wood and splintered glass of the pathetically domestic war-zones, the rows of little blind bricked-up houses from which whole communities have fled, or been expelled, or just drifted away, the evidence of vandalism sifted over with the dust of explosions; all these belie the illusion of neat cleanliness.

Yet the impression of the bird's-eye view is not wholly wrong. Belfast is a working place, where a small Georgian merchant town was transformed in the course of a few decades in the early nineteenth century into a great industrial city, building its prosperity first on linen, then cotton, then linen again, then ship-building and engineering. The linen industry has died now, as have a few other industries more recently established; but ship-building continues. As the city expanded rapidly it drew heavily, of course, on the Ulster countryside for its new population (as well as, to some extent, on nearby Britain). Catholics in large numbers came in, as well as Protestants, and rural conflicts were brought to the city streets. The great Protestant evangelical revival, sometimes called 'the new reformation', which had an impact everywhere in the country in the middle of the nineteenth century, swept Belfast and built up the tensions still higher. Then, as the parliamentary agitation for Home Rule for Ireland, led by Parnell, gained force; as Gladstone introduced the first Home Rule Bill in 1886, rioting between Protestants who were vehemently opposed to coming under a Catholic parliament in Dublin, and Catholics, who hoped to see all remaining Protestant privilege overthrown with Home Rule, became a periodic feature of Belfast life.

But it was to the west of the Bann, in Londonderry, that the recent violence began, in 1968, that was to lead to many years of bloodshed and destruction. Derry, another finely sited, small city, is built, in its central and older part, on a hill that was once an island, washed on its eastern side by the waters of the Foyle as they sweep down into a broad Lough and on to the open sea, and to the west separated from the mainland by a crescentic marsh, on the 'bogside'. Its name means 'oak-grove', and among the trees — and no doubt using their wood — St. Columba built a church in the sixth century. Medieval verses attributed to him praise Derry, the abode of angels.

A large monastery, with a great church, was established on the spot, and flourished. It was in dilapidation, however, by the time of the Elizabethan wars, when the whole north, led by O'Neill (earl of Tyrone according to the English system) and O'Donnell (earl of Tirconnell) rose against the queen. In the later stages of the war, Sir Henry Docwra, making a rear approach to the earls' country by sea, sailed up the Foyle and made a small fortified settlement by the old monastery.

After the defeat of the earls, in the great Plantation of Ulster, the county of Coleraine (later Co. Derry) was given to the London guilds to develop. They renamed it 'Londonderry', girdled the island with walls, and peopled it with Scottish and English settlers.

In the wars of the seventeenth century, when English rebellions and conspiracies had their often unpredictable effects in Ireland, Derry was a Protestant bastion. Politics and religion were inextricable in the seventeenth century. The little city earned its place in myth in 1689. The English had overthrown and banished their king, James II, in favour of his Protestant son-in-law, William of Orange. Ireland, on the whole, remained loyal to James, and he landed in the south to try to retain his throne with Irish help. But the Protestants of Derry and other places declared for King William. Derry, in spite of the incompetence of the Williamite forces that tried to relieve it, and of the faintheartedness of its governor, through the enterprise and endurance of its citizens successfully withstood a siege that had been mounted under the personal command of James II himself.

It is a port, and over its wharves passed a great proportion of those tens of thousands (largely Presbyterians) who emigrated from Ulster to North America in the eighteenth and early nineteenth centuries. They were driven by poverty and religious discrimination (which operated against Presbyterians as well as Catholics, although not as severely, through most of the eighteenth century). They sailed down the Foyle, and, weeks later, up the St. Lawrence, or into Boston harbour or Chesapeake bay. Later, in America, they came to be known as the 'Scotch Irish', and they have left their mark on many parts of the continent, in Canada, in Pennsylvania, in the mountains of Virginia and Kentucky.

By the twentieth century Derry was two-thirds Catholic in its population, while retaining is symbolic historical meaning for Protestants. After partition of Ireland, Derry, the city where the new frontier carved out a tiny half-moon-shaped bridgehead, just beyond its outskirts, on the western shore of the Foyle, was secured to the continued Union, in local electoral politics, by a notorious gerrymander, so that its two-thirds nationalist vote returned a two-thirds unionist representation, and Catholic Derry had a Protestant local government. But a high price can be paid in the end for cheap tricks.

Derry's hinterland is County Donegal, and in particular, the mountainous peninsula between Lough Foyle and Lough Swilly, Inishowen. This takes its name from Eogan, one of the pseudo-historical sons of Niall of the Nine Hostages. Niall was reckoned, with the aid of a good deal of bogus genealogy, to be the ancestor of most of the dominant dynasties in the petty kingdoms of the northern and north midland parts of Ireland in early historic times. The groups known as Uí Néill, or descendants of Niall, expanded their power eastward across Ulster in the early centuries of the Christian period, and two major kingdoms emerged, bearing the names of Niall's sons, Tír Eogain (Tyrone) and Tír Conaill (Tirconnell).

The chief royal centre of the north was on a high hill at the narrowest part of the Inishowen peninsula, from which it commanded a fine view of both Foyle and Swilly. This was Ailech, just a few kilometres from Derry, where traces of a hill-fort, very likely of pre-Christian date, may still be seen, and where the fine stone fort known as the Grianán probably represents a later period, when the Uí Néill dominated the north.

In spite of its early political significance, Inishowen bears from that distant past the imprint of the character not of a king or warrior but of a monk — Columba, or, as he was to be known in the Gaelic tradition, Colum Cille. Although he was not born on the peninsula, but beyond Lough Swilly, this was his country, as its monuments and traditions still testify. Derry, which is (the Border notwithstanding), the chief town of Inishowen, is the place where his memory is still most honoured. He was, however, not merely a monk, but was, as Cremthann (the name by which he was known before he entered religion) a great-grandson of Niall, and, as such, a man eligible for the northern kingship.

His life was remarkable; his medieval legend has a quality of high romance. Bearing responsibility for lost lives, as he had been the occasion of a battle (so it is told), he was enjoined by his confessor to take a boat to sea, and not to settle until he reached land from which he could no longer see Ireland. So he sailed in his curragh from Donegal, and when he first reached land he climbed a hill (perhaps on Islay) and could see the Irish hills shadowy on the far horizon to the south. He sailed on and reached Iona. Ireland can't be seen from there, and there he made his base, and founded the great monastery from which the evangelising of Scotland was undertaken. A poet, he is celebrated in medieval poems:

> There is a grey eye
> That will look back
> Toward the men of Ireland
> And the women.

The current Northern ireland violence began in October 1968 in Derry, when the R.U.C. batoned a comparatively small civil rights march, and rioting ensued. So much has happened since, including two and a half thousand deaths in the following seventeen years, and many more thousands of people maimed, that, at first glance, what was at issue then seems to have little in common with the confused issues of the later bloody conflict. But the turmoil centred on the revolt of a section of the people of Northern Ireland and on the opposition of a section of the population both to British rule and to the rule of the subordinate parliament and government in Belfast that the British had set up in response to unionist refusal to go along with any autonomous or independent government in Dublin.

If we examine the reason for that opposition and place it in the context of modern Irish history as a whole, we can see that in many ways the Ulster problem of today is the Irish problem of yesterday. In other ways it is quite different.

The Irish problem of yesterday lent itself to simplification: as the struggle of the Irish nation against British rule unwillingly endured. But it had other elements. There was a long struggle for 'civil rights'. Catholic Emancipation was promised with the Union with Britain, but, for reasons not anticipated by the parties to that forced bargain, didn't happen until a major political campaign had been undertaken. Other discrimination remained, even after the passing of Emancipation, and the religious majority (as well as some minorities) in Ireland still had cause to campaign against the payment of tithes to the Established Church, and then against Establishment itself. But the Disestablishment Act of 1869, although it concerned mainly an internal Irish matter, was the beginning of the dissolution of the Union. The struggle towards equality of status and opportunity for Irish Catholics was inevitably a struggle, in part, against the British government, which resisted on behalf of the Irish Protestant ascendancy, and became associated therefore to the point of virtual identification, with opposition to the Irish majority. This identification fed nationalism. It had not been quite so in the eighteenth century.

The main difference between that struggle of yesterday and the confused Ulster struggle of the late twentieth century is that — within Ireland — the earlier struggle was one of a majority of the population against a privileged minority. Within the United Kingdom, of course, it was always the resistance of a minority to a system which they felt placed them at a disadvantage. And the minority in question was sustained by its consciousness of being a nation.

But there is much to suggest that, granted a benevolent neutrality within Ireland on the part of the British government, there were times when a great part of the Irish Catholics would have tolerated the Union, provided their numbers within the island would enable them to win the place in society to which they came to believe these numbers entitled them. When, in an older and different political climate, institutional group might negotiate with institutional group in the formation of a political community, or 'social contract', the claims to equality of the Catholics might seem reasonable rather than alarming. But as modern 'democratic' ideas became gradually more and more accepted in the course of the nineteenth century, the mere counting of heads became more and more important. This meant that granting full equal rights to Catholics meant majority *rule*, which meant Catholic domination. Home Rule, in this sense, would no longer (as in the time of the eighteenth-century Dublin parliament) mean autonomy for the previously dominant group in the country, but the entry to office and power of a new group: what the Unionists came to fear as 'Rome rule'.

As it happened, the ascendancy, which of course not only supported the Union and English domination of Ireland but also depended on the British connection for the survival of its own privileged position, was unable in the end to resist the efforts, renewed at frequent intervals and in different areas of life, made by the mass of Catholics to improve their position in Ireland. The Northern Protestants, however, forming an alliance across the divides of religious denomination and social and economic class, were able to maintain a successful rersistance.

The struggle which had gone on for a hundred years now took on a very different character. With partition it divided. The Catholics of the twenty-six-county state followed through on their victory, with moderation although with little tact or real tolerance, being in a position to take the achievement of full equality easily, since time and numbers were on their side.

Within the new state, in time, the struggle subdivided. As the ascendancy dwindled to impotence and unimportance, other issues must and did emerge. Within the North, neither group adjusted very readily to the sudden reversal of its numerical minority-majority status. The Protestant unionists feared, and the Catholic nationalists expected, a return to Irish political unity under Dublin rather than Westminster. Allowing for a long lull caused by demoralisation of a generation of Northern nationalists by their sudden abandonment in 1921, the nineteenth-century struggle continued, but in topsy-turvy fashion.

The confusion between the two themes — which we might describe from their early manifestations as 'Catholic Emancipation' on the one hand and 'Repeal of the Union' on the other — became greater than ever. What has now come to be widely known as the 'minority' in Northern Ireland (where almost all descriptive or interpretative political terms beg questions) directed a struggle on the one hand against discrimination exercised by local Protestant unionist rule, and a struggle on the other hand against British rule and towards Irish union.

The one struggle, however, was wholly within their competence, as being concerned exclusively with the politics of the area within which they were operating. The other involved not only the politics of the existing sovereign Irish state but the assumption by the Northern nationalists of a right to speak and act on behalf of the Irish nation as a whole. These could only be reconciled by full agreement with the authorities of the Irish state to act in concert with them. Such agreement was not achieved, except very briefly and incompletely, when Mr Lynch's government in 1969 gave tentative support to the Ulster uprising but then reneged on its own actions and agents.

On the whole, since the outbreak of violence in Northern Ireland, Dublin governments have chosen rather to re-enact, in a sense, the role of the old Irish parliamentary party at Westminster and attempt to further Irish national aims by negotiating with the British government, more or less as a client, arguing a case for British action — in particular British action to coerce the Northern loyalists.

The Northern nationalists, meantime, have for the most part adopted both constitutional tactics and an armed and violent movement of force, just as the nationalist agitation of the beginning of the century did throughout the island. Since this force was plainly not necessary for the securing of civil rights, it can only be regarded as an appeal to the weight of numbers, in the island as a whole, for the achievement of nationalist, or more accurately Catholic, domination of the Protestant government of Northern Ireland just as domination was achieved finally at the expense of the old ascendancy when Dublin changed hands in 1922. It is not a seventeenth-century religious war, as it is often made out to be, but a nineteenth-century war.

But much of the imagery of the conflict derives from seventeenth-century themes. Ever since the 'final solution' of the Irish question was arrived at in the Treaty of Limerick in 1691, the event has been commemorated and the achievement of the British ascendancy in Ireland has been asserted in annual parades, to the sound of fifes and drums, and to the accompaniment of banners and triumphal emblems. This was far from being exclusively an Ulster phenomenon, and long before the Orange Order was founded in County Armagh, the display of the colour orange figured in such parades and other manifestations as a symbol of the Williamite victory over the Jacobites and of loyalty to the house of Hanover.

Such displays of loyalty to the dynasty that ruled in and from England took on, from time to time in the eighteenth century, a forceful and military character, especially in the north of Ireland. For example, in 1715 and 1745, the years in which Jacobite restorations were attempted in Britain, companies of volunteers from Belfast and other centres were armed and marched out to defend the shores of Ireland, from the invasion of Highlanders which was anticipated on those occasions in support of the Old Pretender or of 'Bonnie Prince Charlie'. On other occasions, the same bodies of subjects who paraded regularly on the anniversary of the battle of the Boyne, armed themselves and marched out with their weapons when England was at war with France and there was a danger of invasion from that quarter.

The Crown which the northerners on such occasions armed to defend was seen by them then, as it still is today, as a symbol and guarantee of their liberties. Then, as now, their position was often paradoxical, or seemingly so. Their loyalty was not to any British *government*, but to the Constitution, or rather to the idea of civil and religious liberty. In 1757, for example, it was the County Antrim Patriot Club, a body formed to foster the independence of the people of the North, which formed a company of armed volunteers for defence against the French. They contributed to the defence of Belfast against the French forces under Thurot who landed in Antrim three years later and seized Carrickfergus.

Liberty, when arms were taken up in its cause, could be defended against others besides the French. In the words of George Benn, an early historian of Belfast, "'The Revolution of 1688'', "the First of July 1690" (i.e. the anniversary of the battle of the Boyne, in the old-style calendar), "the Protestant interest all the world over", flowed from the same lips which upheld the rights of the American colonies to unlimited freedom, and the names of some of the greatest democrats that ever flourished to unlimited applause'.

When France took up the cause of the insurgent American colonies in 1778, Belfast again formed a company of volunteers to defend Irish shores against the French, but this time the same men who armed in support of the British crown had strong sympathy with the struggle of the Americans for liberty. Indeed, on the far side of the Atlantic, a great many Ulstermen, many of whom had emigrated only within the preceding decade, were struggling in arms against the same Crown. The paradox of loyalists firing on the Union flag, which has been remarked on from time to time, is not a new one.

The time of the Volunteer movement of the late eighteenth century, a movement which had its greatest strength in the north, was the first heyday of commemorative marching in Ulster. In 1780, Lord Charlemont inspected a great review of Volunteers on July 12. This commemoration of the Boyne went on in fact for two days, with elaborate manouevres which included a mock battle, in the presence of thirty thousand people, in the Falls Meadows. The parade of July 12, 1784, included a special demonstration in support of the rights of Catholics. In 1791, the Volunteers, accompanied by other groups of Belfast citizens, held their parade not on the anniversary of the Boyne, but on that of a much more recent event, the fall of the Bastille two years before. On July 14 the great procession, with banners and emblems, went through the streets of Belfast. They carried portraits of Mirabeau and of Benjamin Franklin,

Franklin's with the motto, 'Where Liberty is, *there* is my country'. A group from Templepatrick and Carnmoney carried a banner with the slogan, 'Our Gallic brother was born July 14, 1789. Alas! we are still in embryo'. An address was sent to the French National Assembly expressing the joy and sympathy of the people of Belfast at the efforts of the French people. Another address proclaimed that people of different religions should be equal before the law.

In those days, just before the founding of the Orange Order, 'orange' demonstrations, that is demonstrations by people who honoured the achievement of liberty from religious tyranny and royal absolutism, were fully compatible with sympathy for the American and French revolutions — a sympathy which was soon and readily translated into republican sentiments by some.

It was not long after this, however, that formal parades and processions, especially on the anniversary of the Boyne, became a matter of sect and faction. The bitter struggles for land, in mid-Ulster especially, brought out the hostility between Protestant and Catholic which had been latent and which various libertarian and egalitarian movements of the late eighteenth century had tried to do away with. In spite of the United Irishmen and their fraternal and democratic proclamations, the political question in Ireland became, not one which concerned the rights and liberties of all the people, but the question whether the country was to be under Protestant government or, ultimately, Catholic. That question hasn't yet been answered finally in Ulster.

At the other end of the island, the province of Munster in the south has in some ways more claim to distinctiveness than Ulster. Munster is a province of great diversity, broken up by many ranges of hills into a variety of different landscapes. The east-west Armorican folds of its southern parts run westward to the Atlantic in long narrow peninsulas between drowned valleys, with hilly spines separating glen from glen; in its northern parts its fertile plains, between more widely spaced ranges of hills, fade away northward into vast bogs, through which the Shannon flows to the sea. Parts, of west Munster in particular, have escaped, by a functional remoteness, whole phases of Irish cultural history, especially in prehistoric times.

The ancient centre of the province lay well inland, in the plains of south Tipperary, at Cashel. Cashel is an isolated high flat-topped rock, rising abruptly from the plain. It is crowned with a serration of ruined gables and towers and, seen from a distance suddenly coming into view, it is a sight to lift the heart and the imagination, especially of a Munster person.

Unlike the other major royal sites it appears to have no pagan or prehistoric past. The seat of Christian kings for centuries, it was given to the church in 1101, and the ruined buildings upon it date from after that — some from immediately afterwards. They include a round tower, or belfry, probably built just after the church took over, an elaborately carved Romanesque church that was built by Cormac MacCarthy between 1127 and 1134, when he was king of Munster, and a cathedral of something more than a hundred years later. Here was held, on the rock, the synod, summoned by Henry II, that gave the first acknowledgment by a national assembly (of the church) to the English lordship of Ireland.

But after that acknowledgment, Cashel's importance soon dwindled. Munster was early and well penetrated by Norman adventurers, and within decades a new hybrid and fruitful culture was founded in its broad valleys and among its hills. The new Norman lords introduced French literature, music and dance, all of which over the centuries were to make a deep impression on the province; they intermarried with the Irish, fostered their children with them according to the old Irish custom, and came to learn as much as they taught. In the castles and halls of medieval Munster, Irish wit matched continental grace; the harp and the lute made harmony.

Munster's modern capital, insofar as the term can be used, is the city of Cork. It too has a hybrid development in its past. Where the Lee flowed among marshy islets into a fine sheltered harbour, an early monastery was founded; later the Vikings founded a small town on the site. In early modern times this expanded into a great provisioning port, through which the produce of the agriculture of Munster was to flow, largely to the armies, fleets and colonies of the burgeoning British empire. The trade fostered a crop of merchant princelings, and stamped a character on Cork, a place of bargaining intelligences. It teeters on the edge between large village and small city — never just a town — with furious dispute, intense self-regard and incessant gossip.

But with its variation and diversification of landscape, Munster has half a dozen regional capitals: Limerick, which commanded the trade, ancient and once heavy, which entered the Shannon mouth; Waterford, at the other end of the province, commanding the trade that entered the river system of the south-east, and again an important medieval port; Tralee, Ennis, Clonmel, Thurles, and other sub-regional capitals.

In the Middle Ages Munster was the centre of a flourishing hybrid culture — Hiberno-Norman. The model village of Adare in Co. Limerick provides a microcosm of it. Áth Dara, the oak ford, was on the river Maigue, one of the streams which flow northward through the Limerick plain to join the Shannon at its mouth. This was once a well-wooded countryside, with good hunting and good land, and it was early overrun by the Anglo-Normans. Geoffery de Marisco apparently held lands at or near Adare. It was he who founded the house of knights of St. John, or

Hospitallers, which gave the nearby village of Hospital its name. And the extensive de Burgh possessions came to include sites along the Shannon itself, at Castleconnell and Carrigogunnell. In connection with this occupation, numerous fortifications were erected in the region. At first, no doubt, these were of earth and timber, but in due course stone castles were put up, to stand as lasting monuments to the invaders.

At Adare itself a fine stone castle was built at the beginning of the thirteenth century. It is probably the oldest of the antiquities now to be seen there, standing on the bank of the stream within the walled Dunraven estate. It appears not to have been constructed on an earthen Norman motte, but possibly on a more ancient Irish rath, which was used as the basis for the inner ward. If so, the castle-builders modified the ditch of the rath, excavating it deeper and linking it with the stream so that it would form a water-filled fosse. Then they constructed a square keep in the defensive wall which they built along the perimeter of the rath. This was linked by a water-bridge-gate with a large outer ward. Two stone halls were built along the river side of the ward; they now frame the vista along the golfing greens in the estate, which is closed by the elegantly grouped ruins of a Franciscan friary.

While the castle was probably built by de Marisco, and possibly on the site of an earlier Irish fortress, the family chiefly responsible for Adare's great wealth of medieval stonework was that of the Kildare Geraldines. The Marisco lands reverted to the crown and came into the hands of the FitzGeralds, and the Earls of Kildare partly rebuilt the castle and founded and endowed the religious houses which clustered around it. Of these the most complete is that of the Franciscans, founded in 1464. This is an excellent example of the Irish late Gothic style of the west, with its slender tapering square tower, and its close grouping of domestic buildings around the narrow church. The cloister is mostly of the type in which the wall of the ambulatory facing on to the little garth is pierced with arched openings, but one range has a pillared arcade. The kitchen, refectory and other domestic buildings still stand, the church, apart from its roof, is more or less intact, and the whole building fulfils the promise which it offers as one walks across the green lawns towards it. it is, however, only one of a number of fine medieval buildings in the village.

And from Adare, one can visit a countryside full of vestiges of the Hiberno-Norman civilization of the late Middle Ages, the civilization which has contributed as much as any of the others which have come and gone to the shaping of Ireland. Askeaton, Croom, Hospital, Kilmallock; all can show such traces. A few miles to the west is the rath of Ardagh, where a splendid chalice (with other objects) was found to testify to an earlier flowering of culture; a few miles to the east is Lough Gur, on whose shores, apart from further Norman antiquities, were found extensive

Detail of the Giant's Causeway, Co. Antrim

A megalithic chamber, Carrowmore, Co. Sligo

Knocknarea, Co. Sligo

"The Cross of the Scriptures", Clonmacnoise

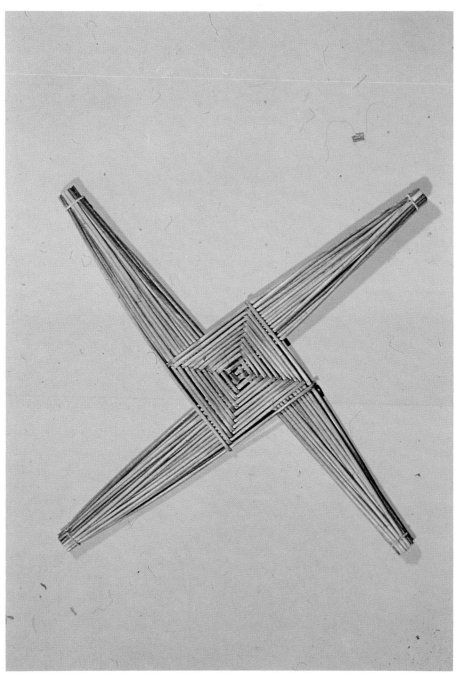

A Kildare type St. Brigid's rush cross

evidence for Neolithic settlement — occupation by the early farmers who laid the first foundations for the long continuity of human living and working in the Limerick countryside.

A school of Gaelic poetry flourished in this area in the eighteenth century. It is still the home of traditional music. The village itself was laid out as an estate village in the early nineteenth century, with cottages and houses designed in the style then fashionable for such a plan, a style designed to suggest the pre-industrial rural past (English rather than Irish) and offered in pattern-books to landlords who wished to prettify their villages with old-world charm. The landlords here were a family with architectural talents and taste, the Quins, whose home had been in Adare since the seventeenth century and who had been Earls of Dunraven since the late eighteenth century. One of the nineteenth-century earls extended his interests beyond the old masonry of his own estate and produced two splendid volumes, still very useful, entitled, modestly, *Notes on Irish Architecture*. They form the first extended work on their subject to be illustrated by photographs. Very fine photographs they are too; some of them have not been surpassed. The work deals chiefly with Ireland's pre-Norman buildings, and it is really a joint work, since it was seen through the press posthumously, by Margaret Stokes, of the Dublin suburb of Rathmines, who was a brilliant pioneer herself in the study of early Irish art.

The Gaelic tradition in poetry and music which flourished at one time round the Maigue spanned the Shannon estuary, and was also vigorous in Co. Clare. In Clare, the Irish tradition survived perhaps in greater depth and variety than in any other county, but the Irish language has finally died within the last generation along the rocky coast that looks out to the Aran Islands. That is to say, that there are no more native speakers of Irish. Clare, 'the banner county', was in the van in modern political movements, returning O'Connell and de Valera to parliament in famous elections.

Leinster is the province which for the longest period has had connections overseas particularly with Wales and England. Its coasts were studded with Viking settlements and, in due course, trading towns. Waterford, a Munster city which is only a river's breadth from Leinster, may be included. These bases became the English bases of medieval Ireland, but retained their own very definite colonial-Irish character. In them the Irish institution of parliament developed parallel to the English institution. The parliaments of the Lordship, later the Kingdom of Ireland, found themselves regularly in disagreement and dispute with the parliaments of the Kingdom of England down many centuries. They met in Dublin, in Drogheda or in Kilkenny.

Leinster, the south-east, also has the advantage in what is crucial in Irish climate: rainfall. It is the driest part of Ireland, where wheat can be grown — especially in periods of comparatively warm climate, the last of which was in the thirteenth century. At that time Leinster became the solid base for a process which was to be checked for a century or two but then was to be overwhelming, the Anglicisation of Ireland. The Laigin, or Leinster, of the early historic period was much smaller than the present province, as its boundaries are now defined, which includes what was then the middle province, *Mide*.

Modern Leinster, with east Ulster, is by far the most densely populated part of the island. This is a major demographic feature of the country in recent times: a marked eastward population shift. In 1800, the total population of Ireland was about what it is now, roughly five million people, but they were much more evenly distributed. Ireland has still, by western European standards, a very low population density, but this is largely because of the comparative emptiness of the country, especially west of Bann and Shannon. More than two million people live along the east coast, from Waterford to Larne. The other three million are, again very unevenly (for most of *them* are still east of Bann and Shannon, or in the far south) distributed over all the rest.

It follows that the province of Connacht is the empty province. And this is so. The whole west, from Donegal to Kerry, is characterized by beautiful but lonely wild landscapes. The observant eye can notice many traces of a once comparatively dense rural settlement in quite remote parts, but this was at the time of the subsistence economy of the potato, and has long ended. A new localised density has reflected certain modern developments, in transport, tourism, and holiday habits, producing, for example, a singularly unpleasant ribbon development for thirty or forty kilometers westward along the coast road from Galway.

Galway itself, a small city with a port and a university, is generally regarded as the capital of Connacht. Nowadays it is also regarded, in a sense, as the capital of the Irish-speaking areas (although it is not in one: they boast no cities), but through the Middle Ages it was an English town, a bridgehead in the west. The inner parts of the town still follow the street plan laid out by the merchant families, or 'tribes', of medieval times, and here and there there are buildings which still include fifteenth or sixteenth-century masonry; but modern Galway takes its character somewhat more from the Irish speaking fishing village, that was once outside its walls, than from the old burghers. And takes still more of its contemporary character from tourists.

As does the west as a whole. Tourism is a major business for Ireland. On the whole, the country survives the business quite well, although it is a dubious and dangerous industry for a small under-developed country to develop as a main source of revenue, since, if overdone, tourism inevitably becomes a corrupting, debasing, and coarsening force: the commercialisation of friendliness and hospitality. This has not quite happened.

The ancient centres of Connacht were not in what are now the main tourist areas, in the west (which were even more thinly inhabited then than now), but in the lowlands of the east, along the Shannon and in its basin. The chief centre at the dawn of history was the land of rolling pastures and low hills around ancient Cruachain, in north Co. Roscommon, and later centres were developed, still east of the Connemara mountains and bogs, at Cong, and at Tuam, which became ultimately the ecclesiastical capital of the western province.

The four provinces of Ireland, non-existent as political entities, exist as realities of the Irish imagination, self-perception and sense of place. Ulster, Munster, Leinster and Connacht may not quite mean war, art, wealth and learning, respectively, to the Irish minds of today, but they still convey, as it were, different nuances, different flavours. A Dublinman myself, I have no very special feeling for Leinster, but, a Munsterman in my bones. I feel a lifting of the heart when, travelling south across the midlands, I cross a low ridge and see on the southern skyline the blue range of the Silvermines or the Galtees in Tipperary, and know that I am entering the real Ireland. And, *mutatis mutandis*, that is how the Irish feel about their provinces.

8
TIME OUT OF TIME

Dr. Kevin Danaher has argued, on the basis of the study of folk-customs, particularly calendar customs, that much in folk tradition comes down to us from a remote pre-Celtic past. This is probably true of the custom of assembly in special places at special times. For example, Ireland shares with Great Britain and the nearby parts of western France a complex of Bronze Age (and some earlier) megalithic monuments, of the types known as 'stone circles' and 'henges' in the language of the archaeologists, which are usually interpreted as ceremonial religious centres.

Stonehenge, on Salisbury plain in southern England, is the best known of these, but there are many, less elaborate, in parts of Ireland — the 'Giant's Ring', near Belfast, for example, or Beltany Ring in Co. Donegal, the extraordinary complex of rings and alignments that was revealed by peat-cutting at Beaghmore on the mountains of mid-Tyrone, the 'Piper's stones' at Athgreany, Co. Wicklow, the great circle and its smaller outlier at Grange, by Lough Gur, Co. Limerick, and many more. These, almost certainly, were the scenes of periodic tribal or inter-tribal assemblies.

Tribal assembly, perhaps somewhat different in character, was a Celtic custom too, and the tradition would have been reinforced by the advent of Celtic traditions in Ireland in the centuries immediately before the time of Christ. The great periodic assembly of early historic times was called an 'oenach', aonach in the modern form — still the Irish word for a fair or market. At the aonach of early times, which lasted for several days, peace was enjoined on all who participated, and there were games, horse-races, or other ritualised celebrations.

More than most other western peoples, the Irish have retained the significance of assembly in their lives, as well as much in their outlook on work and leisure (often unconscious) in which they differ somewhat from their neighbours. Irish people have always been hard workers; and Irish workers laid much of the foundations of the infrastructure of modern Britain and America — digging the British canals in the eighteenth century (the work was done by 'navigators', or 'navvies'), building the railroads, and playing a large part in Britain during and after the Second World War, in building the airfields.

But, except in part in the north-east, what has come to be known — on the basis of rather arbitrary arguments — as 'the Protestant work ethic' —

has not taken root in Ireland. No idolatrous obeisance, generally speaking, is paid to work as such. It could be said, a little fancifully perhaps, that the Irish today, like the Celts of old, count time in nights, not days. Real life begins in the evening. Work was accepted and endured as part of the human condition, but as a part derived from the primeval curse: 'In the sweat of thy face shalt thou eat bread'.

The volume of traffic on the streets of Irish towns, or on the roads of the countryside, doesn't grow heavy until a much later hour in the morning than on the Continent, or even in Britain. But people don't retire so early in the evening. Society, social life, is the spiritual sustenance of people, and the day, the week and the year are marked by gatherings. In the countryside the great frequent regular meeting place is the church. After Sunday Mass, the people who have gathered in from miles around linger outside the church, some of them, increasingly in recent years, adjourning to the pubs, which open as Mass ends, to discuss the news of the week, the state of the crops or the prices, the minutiae of politics. Less frequent, but more prolonged gatherings take place for periodic cattle-marts or fairs. People come, some quite long distances, in the morning from their often scattered and isolated farms, to sell or buy beasts and produce; but, as much, to patronise the shops of the town, and the pubs, where they can spend a busy day engaged in the life-craft of the Irish, the craft of words.

Small Irish villages and towns strike the visitor to the country by the number of public houses to be seen, in what is often not much more than one long street, where every other door seems to have a beer advertisement hanging over it. Many of these, however, are shops — greengrocers, tailors, hardware merchants, confectioners, who sell beer and spirits at a small bar, often in the dark recesses at the back of the building. Most hours of most days little such business is done. Such towns are in the tradition of the old assembly places. They truly function fully only at intervals of two or three weeks when the streets and the pubs fill with men and women from the hinterland.

Certain types of assembly are much less widespread now than they were in the early nineteenth century. Once, the whole country was filled with ancient church sites, holy wells, and other special places, where people gathered in large numbers on special occasions, most commonly annually, on the festival day of the 'patron' or founder of the church. Sometimes the patron, or 'pattern' celebrations would last for several days and be accompanied by drinking, dancing, selling, and other activities as well as praying — activities which could include, for example, the abduction of likely looking young women. These surely carried on much of the tradition of the ancient *aonach*. Within those two or three decades, a crucial period, just before the great famine of the 1840s, the Catholic church in a great many places worked to put an end to such customs. A similar drive was renewed after the famine, embracing more local and frequent assembly customs, such as cross-roads dancing.

For the Catholic church organisation, painfully built up through the eighteenth century, under the pressure of the penal laws, had conducted a long endeavour to transform the religious behaviour and beliefs of the people, bringing them into conformity with the post-Tridentine disciplines of the Counter-Reformation church. By the nineteenth century, the clergy were attempting more than that. In the effort to win for their people an adequate place in the competitive and rapidly changing society of the United Kingdom after the Industrial Revolution, they were doing their best to inculcate the manners, morals and outlook that would make Irish people more acceptable to the stern and 'sincere' evangelical Protestantism that prevailed at the time. Some of the quality of recent Irish Catholicism, notably its puritanism, may be attributed to this.

The significance of religion in present-day Ireland is often related to the heritage of early Christian times. But it is doubtful if the modern manifestation can be explained so. There are too many gaps to fill in the long record of the centuries: the continuities are very tenuous indeed. But it is undoubted that religion has an importance in people's lives, and effects their public attitudes — and still, to a large extent, their private behaviour — much more than is usual in the western world today.

Traditionalism too is a marked element of Irish religion. St Patrick, who lived fifteen hundred years ago, has a legend which is still living. Even to the present day pilgrims throng to places associated with his legend. Thousands every year undergo severe penitential exercises on the island in Lough Derg in County Donegal which was the site famous in the Middle Ages as the mouth of Hell and which was and is known as 'St Patrick's Purgatory'.

Another remarkable annual pilgrimage is that to Croagh Patrick, the Mayo mountain up which as many as 50,000 people toil on a Sunday in late July each year:

'And Patrick reached the mountain of Aighle, on which he fasted for forty days and forty nights, following the discipline of Moses and Christ; his charioteer died in Muirisc Aighle, that is the plain between the mountain and the sea. And he buried that most devoted charioteer, and heaped up a cairn of stones, and said: "Remain here for eternity, and in the last days I will visit you again".

And then Patrick went from there up to the mountain peaks at the summit of Cruachan Aighle, and there he remained for forty days and forty nights. And great birds came before him, so numerous that he could not see the face of the heavens or of the sea: these represented the souls of all the saints of Ireland, past, present and future. God said: "Go up, holy man, on to the peak which overlooks all the mountains of the western world, to bless the peoples of Ireland", so Patrick saw, as it were, the fruit of his labours, that is, the chorus of all the saints of Ireland coming to visit him, their father.'

The words written thirteen hundred and more years ago, in one of the earliest accounts of Patrick's mission, are remembered. That continuity exists. And, even in its earliest days, there was something distinctive about the Irish and Scottish church, a church, in the seventh, eighth and ninth centuries, of ascetic monks. One of its distinctive features was a particular kind of intransigence, a reluctance to change, combined with a great certainty of the rightness of Irish ways and Irish traditions. Probably the earliest Irish man whose words we possess and whose mind in some sense we can come to know was the monk Columbanus, who worked in Gaul and Italy at the end of the sixth century. Round about the year 600 he was in correspondence, among others, with several popes: 'Watch, for the water has now entered the vessel of the church, and the vessel itself is in perilous straits. For all we Irish, inhabitants of the world's edge, are disciples of Saints Peter and Paul and of all the disciples who wrote the sacred canon by the Holy Spirit, and we accept nothing outside the evangelical and apostolic teaching. None has been a heretic, none a Judaizer, none a schismatic; but the Catholic faith, as it was delivered by you first, who are the successors of the Holy Apostles, is maintained unbroken.'

Columbanus, trained at the monastery of Bangor in County Down, speaks with a voice which would not seem strange coming from many an Irish churchman of the twentieth century. In the twelfth century Ireland became a province of the west-European church. The 'Celtic church' (so called in modern times) came to conform to continental and English ways. The Anglo-Norman settlement in Ireland reinforced this change. To some extent the church lost its former vigour and individuality in religious matters. The Tudor conquests, the Reformation, the wars of religion and the plantations reinforced the intransigent and conservative character of religion in Ireland. It became the badge of political and cultural allegiance as well as the expression of ancient tradition.

Confrontation, sectarianism, partisanship, intolerance, have marked much in Irish religion down to recent times. They too have strengthened conservative tendencies. Neither Protestantism nor Catholicism has been particularly open to ideas. What mattered was right belief, rather than adventurous thinking, however responsible. For example, in 1932, when the Christian churches in Ireland were celebrating the fifteenth centenary of St Patrick's coming, Cardinal MacRory excluded Protestants from a right to take part in the celebrations. He pointed out that their churches were 'not even a part of the Church of Christ'.

'I have no ill-feeling towards non-Catholics', he said later. 'I never said a word against non-Catholics. What I did say, and what gave offence to many, was against their churches and not against themselves'. On the opposite side from such Roman Catholic intransigence (not so common now as in 1932) there is the fundamentalist spirit, especially in Ulster. It falls back frequently on eighteenth- or nineteenth-century works of Protestant apologetics:

'If Rome be indeed the Babylon of the Apocalypse, and the Madonna enshrined in her sanctuaries be the very Queen of Heaven, for the worshipping of whom the fiery anger of God was provoked against the Jews in the days of Jeremiah, everyone must shudder at the thought of giving such a system the least countenance of support'.

In the twelfth century Ireland had been opened up to the outside world. There was a chance that the seventeenth and eighteenth centuries it might be opened up again. To some extent it was. Eighteenth-century Dublin, handsome, elegant and enlightened, contrasted with the backward-looking and inward-looking hinterland. New ideas spread from the east coast. For a while too the little eighteenth-century city of Belfast was a centre of liberalism in religion and politics and of new (mainly French) ideas.

But the immigrants who came to seventeenth-century Ulster, including many Scottish Presbyterians, had a way of life more like that of the defeated Irish than that of the new Protestant upper and middle class of Dublin. They were hardworking, poor, discriminated against by the Establishment. Many were involved in the great republican uprising of 1798, which was savagely put down. By the 1820s and 1830s the change from a liberal and open spirit in Presbyterianism to an illiberal, conservative and closed spirit was well advanced. Presbyterianism moved rapidly away from its liberal, republican, and radical past towards a Toryism which ran to sectarian extremes in the New Reformation of the middle of the nineteenth century. Fear became the strait-jacket of Irish religion. Irish political divisions deepened along sectarian lines. Protestantism froze into a posture of unyielding defence. Mass movements among the great Roman Catholic majority in nineteenth century Ireland grew in strength and fed Protestant fears.

In the nineteenth century too Irish Roman Catholicism assumed a distinctive form, which largely received its stamp from the national seminary at Maynooth. This form derived from the essence of the compromise which was made with the British government. The men trained at Maynooth, for example, by and large taught people to respect the state institutions in the country. By and large also they conformed in many ways to the pattern or the character of nineteenth-century England — one might even say of nineteenth-century English Protestantism.

Maynooth, where the Royal College of St Patrick was founded at the end of the eighteenth century, became a symbol and more than a symbol. For it was from this seminary set among the plains of north Kildare that generations of Roman Catholic priests, trained in its halls and chapel, came to carry out their parochial duties in various parts of the island. In the classrooms of Maynooth the mentality and the outlook of these men (many of them farmers' sons) was formed, and they in turn went all over the country and helped to mould the minds of the people through teaching in the local schools, through sermons and, of course, through the confessional. At Maynooth, the hierarchy meets — the assembly of the Roman Catholic bishops of Ireland — and from there it issues its statements and sometimes its instructions to the faithful. These can be of considerable social significance; an instruction to parents forbidding them to send their children to Trinity College, Dublin (which for many years was particularly strictly enforced in the archdiocese of Dublin itself) had the effect down to the 1960s of maintaining Trinity as a largely Protestant preserve.

For such reasons Maynooth was regarded by many people as a symbol of Roman Catholicism in Ireland and by some as a symbol of conservatism, backwardness and resistance to change. But Maynooth was always much more than this, and quite a few innovations came from it in the past. Its very foundation was a major innovation in the relations between the Roman Catholic church and the state in Ireland. This meant that in the nineteenth century Irish Catholicism assumed a distinctive form — which received its stamp from Maynooth. A certain puritanism and sternness emanated from Maynooth, especially in outward observances, and made its presence felt throughout Ireland in the nineteenth century. Maynooth-trained priests relentlessly broke up many of the cultural patterns of medieval and early-modern Ireland — pattern days, pilgrimages, crossroads dancing, drinking, sexual licence of one kind or another (all of them inter-related) came under disapprobation. By the end of the nineteenth century Roman Catholicism in Ireland had much more of a Protestant look about it in many ways than Roman Catholicism in Mediterranean Europe.

It is quite different from the Catholicism of Spain or Italy or Portugal. The very architecture of Maynooth was, in part at least, some of this story; the Gothic-Revival buildings would be at home in England. In some ways Maynooth certainly was conservative. having established a pattern, it tried to maintain it. Maynooth had this much in common with Protestant Belfast, that ways of thinking and behaving which were set in the early nineteenth century were carried on right into the middle of the twentieth century. All changed in the decade or so after the second Vatican Council. Maynooth was opened to women and to lay people, as a university college, and became for a while a centre of such radical movements as occurred in so many universities in the western world in the sixties and early seventies.

We need to find an explanation for conservatism insofar as it existed among Roman Catholics and dissenters. They were long excluded from government and from full participation in the political life of the country. Fear, combined with promises and half-promises, made them wary of radical change. Among Presbyterians, the very democratic structure of the church has reinforced this tendency to the present day. Ministers are, to a large extent, at the mercy of the most reactionary people in their congregations — who can generally sway the rest when outside danger is apprehended (as it permanently is among Ulster Protestants). Ministers who move too far (and that is not very far) in the direction of liberalism or tolerance are cast out. As a result, Presbyterianism has largely reversed the character it once held.

There was an established church in Ireland for a long time, the Church of Ireland, brought under the Union to be part of the Church of England and Ireland. However the established church in Ireland could never enjoy the same confidence in its position as the Church of England. Romeward tendencies, which might be indulged in English circumstances, were dangerous in Ireland, where the church maintained a privileged position among the great discontented mass of Roman Catholics. Experiment was not encouraged. The Church of Ireland remained 'low'. Change was resisted. It slowly gave ground on Catholic Emancipation, but not without an output of pamphlets and books that make very nasty reading now. It was unwilling to relinquish the payment of tithes.

Finally, Disestablishment came in 1869. The Land Acts which deprived of their landed wealth and political power proprietors who were mainly of the Anglican faith, the rise of *Sinn Féin* and the setting-up of the Irish Free State, the steep decline in Protestant numbers in the new twenty-six-county state (largely due to the strict Roman Catholic rules on intermarriage between Catholics and Protestants): all have combined to create a situation in which a natural reluctance to welcome change might be expected. Up to now, if there has been agreement on little else between the churches, there has been agreement, north and south of the Border, on segregation in education. And in the eighties there has been a marked swing back to old conservative attitudes among Catholic church leaders.

Change comes slowly in these matters to the community as a whole. A decline in church-going is obvious but is very difficult to measure. In spite of it the Irish, Catholic and Protestant, on both sides of the Border, continue to be Europe's most diligent attenders at religious services. In 1983 a referendum was held in the Republic to amend the Constitution so that no law could be passed to permit abortion. The existing law prohibits abortion, but some extreme groups, who detected a drift towards secular liberalism and agnosticism in the country, pressed for the amendment, to guard against the very possibility of a change in the law. The amendment was carried, by a popular vote of two to one.

But the vote will bear analysis, in view of the perceived drift to liberalism. The church, through the pulpits, threw its weight on the side of the amendment. But the poll — just about half the number on the register — was extremely low for an Irish vote. A study of the vote, constituency by constituency, gives a rough indication of the distribution of 'yes' and 'no' votes. In urban middle-class areas there was a vote of about two to one *against* the amendment. Urban working-class areas conformed to the national average — about two to one for the amendment. Rural areas were overwhelmingly for it, in some cases by five or six to one. Taken in conjunction with the general pattern of demographic change in Ireland, this would suggest that there is indeed a drift towards liberalism, but so far a very slow one, which could well be reversed.

It has not brought the churches together in a common cause, except sporadically and patchily. Catholics and Protestants are taught, play, and grow up separately — forming distinct sub-cultures which, as long as religion forms the dividing line, with its deep-rooted political implications in the Irish context, will be at least suspicious of one another, if not actually hostile, in Northern Ireland in particular. Common ground is shared by those who have moved away from religion, but the churches in Ireland, in spite of the increase in ecumenical meetings, in spite of the changes which have taken place in the world around them, still regard each other in the light, or rather in the darkness, of old suspicions, or even hatreds, many of which have little to do with any religion, but come from out-of-date politics. The prolonged conflict in the North was anticipated in the mid-nineteen-sixties by an outbreak of violence which was associated with, among other matters, the Rev. Ian Paisley's campaign against the ecumenical movement.

There are still a few places where pattern customs are observed today — Ardmore, Co. Waterford, for example, where St. Declan is honoured, or St. MacDara's island, off the Connemara coast in Co. Galway, a sea-borne annual pilgrimage. But most have long since ended. As have the gatherings of ancient pagan tradition, Christianised in the Middle Ages, such as the assemblies that took place on hill-tops all over Ireland, usually on a Sunday at the end of July or beginning of August — the *Festival of Lughnasa* that Maire MacNeill has examined so ably. Among the handful of survivals of this festival of the Celtic god *Lugh*, one is notable: the annual pilgrimage in late July in which thousands of people toil up the slope of Croagh Patrick in Co. Mayo.

But another type of assembly has become common in modern Ireland, and has to some extent displaced some of the older ones. This has its counterparts throughout the modern world: it is the sporting meeting. Horse-racing has long been associated with certain of the ancient gatherings, including the Lughnasa festival. Nowadays it is a ritual in its own right. The breeding and training of hunters and racehorses is an important and firmly established industry. The green plains and slopes of Kildare and Tipperary, in particular, in the midlands, abound with stud-farms, racing stables and the paddocks and white-painted rail fences, within which some of the finest horses in the world are bred and trained.

The Dublin Horse Show, in the first week in August, used to be one of the major international events in the Irish year, as well as being an assembly common to both the Anglo-Irish and the plain Irish. It still has something of this character, although it is of diminished significance in recent years. The Royal Dublin Society, which organises it, is a body founded in the eighteenth century which set itself out to encourage improvements in agriculture, stock-breeding, science and practical knowledge. It has functioned very well for two centuries, but in recent years, perhaps because many of its functions have been taken over by other bodies, mainly state-sponsored, it has lost much of its former vigour.

Soccer, which used to be a game chiefly associated with a limited number of towns, where soldiers were garrisoned, has in Ireland as in so many other parts of the world gained much wider popularity and a following of afficionados in recent decades. But its support is still somewhat patchy. Rugby, overwhelmingly a middle-class game in Ireland, is in some ways more significant. The regular round of international games, between Ireland on the one hand and England, Scotland, Wales and France on the other, in the winter months draws big crowds, many travelling to Dublin, Belfast, Cardiff, Edinburgh, London or Paris to the games. And in the 'triple crown' playoffs, involving only the four countries of the old United Kingdom, a much wider audience than the regular followers of rugby takes an active interest.

But the most important and distinctive sporting system is that nowadays wholly associated with the Gaelic Athletic Association. The chief games played are hurling, a native game of very great antiquity, and Gaelic football, which also has a long tradition of many centuries in Ireland but may possibly derive from the games of the English colonial towns of the Middle Ages.

Hurling, played with stick and ball and with some resemblance to hockey, is the fastest game played on dry land. The *camán* or hurley, may be lifted high and the ball struck in the air. The game requires great skill — which many believe must be acquired in early childhood — and stamina, and can be somewhat dangerous with unskilled players. This is a game which survived best down the ages in the better lands of parts of the south and east. It was sponsored by the gentry in the eighteenth and nineteenth centuries, and was often played between parishes, sometimes between counties. At one time it was a common Christmas Day pastime.

The G.A.A. was founded in 1884, largely with the initial intention of 'democratising' certain kinds of sport, and making them available to artisans and labourers as well as the middle classes and gentry who previously patronised them through somewhat exclusive clubs that had sprung up in Victorian days. The G.A.A. however had an astonishingly rapid success, and very soon became intimately associated with nationalist politics, and, in its early days, the scene of a struggle for control between the parliamentary nationalists and the revolutionary republicans of the Irish Republican Brotherhood. The IRB, on the whole, won, and the GAA became an extremely effective vehicle for the revolutionary politics of the beginning of the century. It was joined by tens of thousands of young men in every part of rural nationalist Ireland, who formed clubs, met regularly for sporting contests between parishes, clubs or counties, and soon developed an ethos — and sets of rules — that excluded those of whom politically they didn't approve. In the countryside in particular it provided for the banding of young men under cover of sport (in which in fact they were active and interested). Today, in Northern Ireland, the GAA is an organisation, virtually exclusively, of the nationalist population.

Its importance for rural Ireland over the past hundred years would be difficult to exaggerate. It has given real meaning in the consciousness of the people to those somewhat arbitrary and late devices of the English administration, the counties. It has been a powerful bonding force, giving a common interest to people throughout the island, and an atmosphere in which intense loyalty to the county team has generally been combined with an open good will towards the opponents (at strictly local level this may not always be so). It has, in other words, been one of the powerful forces making for a sense of common nationality (as distinct from nationalism, although, of course, the two are connected) in modern Ireland.

The old Gaelic custom of the *céilí*, essentially a rural custom, known in Scotland as well as Ireland, has survived, with some transmutation, into contemporary Ireland. The *céilí* was a gathering of the neighbours in one family's house, to spend a night in singing, dancing, storytelling, talking. It was an everyday version of the larger and more formal gatherings associated with rites of passage, waking the dead or attending a wedding.

In urban as well as rural settings, Irish parties often assume the character, or some of it, of the old rural *céilí*. There is a certain ritual. Singing and playing music come at a certain stage of the evening. There is often a considerable formality. There is steady drinking. And the gathering must, to be successful, go late into the night. This is the *real* time, and this is the real activity of life: human communion pushed into the night hours until a light shines through. It is a kind of *agape*, or love-feast, nourished not just on alcohol but also on talk, wit and, ultimately, the intercourse of mind, flesh and spirit. *Lá dar saol*, 'a day of our lives' (usually in fact a night) is the Gaelic expression for the epiphany that comes with such occasions.

The emphasis nowadays is on the verbal arts, but in early times Ireland had several periods of flourishing of highly original forms in visual art, and, now that there is some material base for it, it is always possible that it may do so again. In the Bronze and Iron Ages, workers in gold and bronze, at several periods of intensified activity, turned out work of great sophistication, sometimes splendid and ornate, sometimes simple but beautifully conceived and made.

But the centuries immediately after the introduction of Christianity saw the most elaborately developed and integrated cultural system, in which visual artists, poets, scholars, builders and thinkers lived in the same cosmos with the same terms of reference, and could engage in an interchange which is difficult to understand now — for their world is remote from us, and the workings of their minds are not readily understood.

In periods of isolation, Irish culture has stagnated; in periods of fairly active intercourse with the outside world it has often been stimulated. The stimulation, by a seeming paradox, has been not merely to imitation but, quite rapidly, to originality. Originality comes not from consciously attempting to be different, but rather from persistent efforts to improve on foreign models and adapt them to the needs, tastes and resources of the country.

Many examples of this are provided by the art of the so-called 'golden age' of the seventh, eighth and ninth centuries A.D. This was a time when a vast amount of what was foreign originally was fully assimilated. Christianity had come, already moulded by its development over the first few centuries within the rigid forms of Roman imperial civilization and administration. Its structures and hierarchies were Roman; its thought, language and outlook, in the west, were Roman, with an extensive Greek background. All this could not be absorbed immediately. By the seventh century, however, the process was well advanced: the Irish language had received the respectability of written form; members of leading Irish families had begun to enter and patronise the church; and the steady replacement of an episcopal by a monastic organization marked the steady Gaelicisation of the Roman import.

In the seventh century was added the influence, very significant in art, of the Germanic peoples, whose wanderings, in war-bands and alliances of migrating tribes, had brought them so far west as to be neighbours of the

Irish in Britain and Gaul. In particular, the advent of the Anglo-Saxons in Romano-Celtic Britain had brought Irish artists and craftsmen into contact with a new world of imagination and technique. The pilgrimage or mission of Irish monks overseas made the contacts close and significant, for both the Anglo-Saxons and the Franks, unlike the majority of Germanic tribes (who were mostly Arian Christians when they crossed the frontiers of the Empire) were pagans when they arrived in the west, and soon became the objects of evangelizing activity. The showy polychrome jewellery of the Anglo-Saxons plainly made quite an impression on the Irish, who were greatly stimulated, and added their own versions of interlacings and animal-ornament of the Germanic styles to their own repertoire of design and ornament.

The products of these fruitful contacts are well known today, at least in so far as they have survived the centuries. But the rediscovery of the 'golden age' is a work of comparatively recent times, and is by no means complete yet. When the Royal Irish Academy was founded in Dublin in 1784, it was still widely believed by the savants that pre-Norman Ireland was sunk in barbarism. It was largely under the auspices of the Academy, in the course of the following century that Irish Studies came to throw an abundance of light on that distant period, as well as on more recent phases of the past. And new discoveries were made. In the middle of the nineteenth century both the 'Tara Brooch' and the Ardagh chalice were, accidentally, discovered, while the work of antiquaries and scholars was gradually making known other treasures whose existence had been unknown or forgotten.

For several generations of Irish people after that, the Tara Brooch became almost the chief symbol of the civilization of ancient Ireland, that civilization, as a somewhat over-simple but widely-held view had it then, which had been eclipsed by foreign conquest. The general shape and outline of the brooch have been copied in ten thousand trinkets. It has helped to sell chocolates, insurance and holidays in Ballybunion.

It was found in the middle of the last century, in circumstances which are not altogether clear, on or near the beach near Bettystown, Co. Meath. It came into the hands of a Drogheda jeweller and then to a Dublin jeweller. It has no connection whatever with Tara, but was given the name by which it is still known because this sounded romantic and appropriate. When it first became known to the modern world, therefore, it already had attached to it what were considered suitable associations to link it with the 'golden age', which was dimly known from Tom Moore's lyrics and similar works:

> The harp that once in Tara's halls
> The soul of music shed

Fox hunting with the Galway Blazers

Senior Hurling Final, Croke Park, 1983

Steeple chasing at Gowran Park, Co. Kilkenny

An aerial view of the crowd at the Bob Dylan concert, Slane Castle, Co. Meath, 1984

A street scene from the Fleadh Cheoil at Buncrana, Co. Donegal

Interior of an Irish Country Inn, 19th century print

"The Spaniard", a pub in Kinsale, Co. Cork

Now hangs as mute on Tara's walls
As if that soul were dead.
So sleeps the pride of former days,
So glory's thrill is o'er
And hearts that once beat high to praise
Now feel that pulse no more.

The brooch is quite a small object, its ring being just eight centimeters in diameter. It is made of silver but is richly gilt on the pin and the ring head. What makes the brooch quite remarkable is the profusion of ornament, executed in various techniques, on a minute scale, which covers its surfaces. There are interlacings, intertwined fantastic and distorted animal-forms, animal-head reliefs, elaborate compositions of interlocking spirals, and geometric settings of coloured glass and amber. Every surface is ornamented, and the back of the brooch is slightly more elaborate in its decoration (which is also better preserved) than the front.

The techniques include a very fine filigree, which is used in the main triangular panels on the front of the brooch. The equivalent panels on the back, ornamented with complex spirals, employ a remarkable technique. The patterns were first produced as a fine line relief on copper plates. Molten silver was then washed over the copper and burnished down to leave the fine copper lines of the design set off against the silver ground.

Other pieces came to light to show that this, although rare and costly, was in some sense representative of a whole class of objects and of workmanship and style. Microscopic perfection of work also characterises the Ardagh Chalice, and the hoard of silver ecclesiastical vessels (including another chalice) found in 1980 at Derrynaflan in Co. Tipperary. Every day now hundreds of people file through the library of Trinity College, Dublin, to see the fantastically elaborate and minute whirlings and intertwinings of ornament, and the dozens of tiny drawings of men and beasts, on the enamel-like pages of the Kells Gospels. And the Book of Kells is only one of a number of such sumptuous Gospel books produced at that time.

This is a very strange visual art. The culture which produced it also carved great monumental standing stone crosses, covered with many of the motifs found in the metalwork and the manuscripts, but also with sculptured scenes illustrating biblical and monastic history. But they built small plain churches, beautifully wrought and finished in dressed stone. Possibly they too had elaborate ornament and figured scenes once, painted on a thin skrim of plaster. But carved relief ornament is spare and plain.

It is across a void of centuries that this art, and the remote minds of the people who produced it, came again in the past two hundred years to stimulate and inspire modern Ireland. People no longer go for direct and simple inspiration to that art, as they did a hundred, or even fifty years ago. But we are still learning about the culture of early Ireland, still deciphering its texts, and still recognising, every now and then, that there are real continuities down the long sequence of centuries.

The designs in the different media of the art of that distant time are closely inter-related. It was an integrated culture. But it is quite difficult for us, now, to understand. Manuscript illumination, if one comes to think about it, is, for example, a fairly specialised art. Ireland had something of a reputation, in what are known as 'the Dark Ages', for books. Not, perhaps, for the illuminations, but just for being a place of books, as texts. At that time, of course, printing was the best part of a thousand years in the future, the Roman system of publication, involving a kind of mass production on a handcraft basis, was a thing of the past, and the output of books, all written by hand, must have been very slow indeed.

Not only that: it was costly in other respects. Papyrus was no longer available as a cheap substance to serve as a medium for the written word. Animal skin, specially prepared, was used for writing on, and, while there may have been some more ephemeral media, all our earliest surviving manuscripts are on vellum. Any kind of book took quite a while to prepare, since it had to be done on this expensive material, which in turn was hand-prepared, and since it all had to be laboriously copied out, in ink, or inks, which were themselves hand-made.

In the circumstances, when books were luxury items anyway, it is perhaps not surprising that so many should have been treated as sumptuary objects, their value enhanced by minute and painstaking workmanship. Their value was not monetary (the society in which the manuscripts were produced did not use money) or one to be reckoned in terms of exchange or barter.

It may well be that some manuscripts were treated with a great elaboration of ornament for the glory of God and for no other reason or purpose. But the more elaborate and the more ingeniously ornamented the manuscript, the more in fact it was worth, both in terms of exchange value and in terms of its value as a 'relic' or producer of revenues for a church or shrine. We meet in these works the ambiguity that has characterised religious objects down the ages — for a Gospel book like the Book of Durrow or the Book of Kells was not just a text of the Gospels which had been treated with extraordinary virtuosity of craftsmanship for the glory of God: it was also a valuable possession for the monastery to which it belonged; one which helped to draw pilgrims and offerings.

In other words, the fantastic elaboration of minute workmanship in a product like the Book of Kells may be regarded, under one aspect anyway, as a display of conspicuous waste (in this case, of man-hours and of superlative, if myopic, skill); a demonstration almost in Marxist terms (since the labour-content is what is forced on one's attention) of the value of the object.

When we attempt to judge an object like this aesthetically, we must take into account the fact that a great deal of the value and purpose resides precisely in the demonstration of the consumption of so many man-hours in the production of the work. The Book of Kells is therefore quite unlike such sophisticated works as Japanese prints or Chinese paintings, where the artist is saying to his audience: 'The value of this is that it has taken many years of study and training, as well as certain innate talents, to produce such a superb work of art with a few seemingly careless strokes of the brush'. On the contrary, what the Kells or Lindisfarne artist is saying to the customer (or to God — the principle here is the same) is: 'The value of this work may be seen in the extraordinary difficulty of producing on so minute a scale such precise and accurate geometrical forms — with the hand and pen alone (occasionally aided by a pair of compasses); by the skill and knowledge which can derive from the long decorative tradition of the past, in metal-working, sculpture and other media, the forms which will suit the elaboration of the text of a book; and, finally, and not least, the obviously enormous expenditure of time, diligently spent, which went into the making of these astonishing visual forms'.

Here, perhaps, we have the reason why such works as the Book of Kells are, on the whole, admired more for their virtuosity or ingenuity than for their more strictly aesthetic qualities. One's first instinct is to marvel at the fact that they could be done at all. One's second, perhaps, is to wonder if the initial admiration is not for a kind of circus act, like a dog or an elephant performing on its hind legs.

Kells dazzles with its accomplishment, with its microscopic contrivances, with the perfection of performance in producing accurate spirals, circles and endless other definable and predictable forms on a minute scale. Yet, there is more to it than that. Granted, one soon comes to the conclusion that the work could only have been produced by someone who was steeped in the ornamental traditions of Celtic Christianity, stemming from the Iron Age past but in touch with the decorative arts of the West as a whole; by someone who was wholly dedicated to a display of virtuosity, whether to please the abbot or to please God. But there is more to it. The superb craftsmanship is often betrayed into fussiness or bathos by some demand for over-elaboration which we cannot now quite pin down. But, more often, it manages to overcome demands for mere ostentation.

One of the most striking things about the early illuminated manuscripts, if we come to give them considered examination, is that the virtuosity is so often encompassed in an over-all scheme of composition which achieves, from the equivalent of the Book of Job written on a postage stamp, something basically simple, straightforward and beautiful. This is not always evident even in the best colour reproductions of the manuscripts. These do not, for example, convey the effect of the depth of painting in works such as the Book of Kells, where the paint is laid on in layers to produce a three-dimensional and sculptured effect, as well as a sense of enamelling that cannot be conveyed by printing. They do not convey the depth and translucency of colour. But they do show the beauty of the lettering. And it is in this — the humbler part, it might seem, of the work — that one can find the aesthetic which justifies the extravagance of the illuminations. The page justifies the initials; the ordinary letters justify the fantastic whirligigs of the Chi-Rho. The scribes, if not the painters, were artists.

The elaboration of ornament leaves an impression that Irish art of that time depended on a dizzying intricacy and complexity of pattern. But the impression renders only part of the truth. The taste for a pedantic intricacy of pattern, following a kind of mad logic through bewildering convolutions without making a mistake, was, and perhaps still is, a feature of the Irish temperament. But some of the achievements of the early civilisation obey quite other laws.

Among these is the script, which pleases by simplicity and elegant proportion. It is not confined to the manuscripts. It is to be found on a group of monuments which receives less notice than it deserves, the inscribed gravestones to be found at many early ecclesiastical sites. These are usually thin slabs, most often of sandstone, which were laid on the graves either as simple markers of position or, in developed examples, as a covering for the full length of the grave. The inscriptions themselves are usually short and simple, following one of a few formulae, of which the most common simply asks for 'a prayer (*oroit*) for N . . . ' The word *oroit* is almost invariably contracted in the inscription to $\overline{OR}$, so that the text appears on the slab in the form, to quote one of the many Clonmacnoise examples, $\overline{OR}$ DO THUATHAL, with the mark of contraction shown as a horizontal stroke over the abbreviated word. Sometimes the personal name alone appears, especially on very early examples; sometimes a personal name with a word of description, as in another Clonmacnoise example reading COLMAN BOCHT. This is unique because the word *bocht* (the poor) is written in ogham script. Sometimes there is a simple variation on the basic formula, as in the Iona example which reads $\overline{OR}$ AR ANMAIND FLAIND (a prayer for the soul of Fland) and, rarely, an expansion which tells us something about the dead person other than his profession or calling — as on the Clonmacnoise slab asking a prayer for Feidlimid, which goes on to tell us, in Latin, that he was killed without cause.

The slabs have been the subject of a number of studies. What these show is that, of the many thousands of such grave-slabs that must once have existed, perhaps as many as a thousand still survive, some, however being represented only by small fragments. These span a period of five or six hundred years and can, for purposes of study, be divided into groups representing not only different periods but also different localities. They are a product of monastic culture, European and Latin in their early background, but gradually, as the centuries went by, showing more and more the influence of the indigenous artistic tradition. Wherever numbers of inscribed slabs are found there are other slabs, similar in design and marked with similar Christian symbols, which do not bear inscriptions. It seems probable that some uninscribed grave-markers with Christian symbols are among the very earliest memorials of Christianity in the country.

The high crosses and similar or related carved stones occur in Ireland in a somewhat limited distribution. They are found chiefly in two broad and not very sharply defined bands, the first extending across Ulster as far south as a line from Sligo Bay to the mouth of the Boyne, the second stretching from the coast of Wicklow and Wexford to the area around Galway Bay. High crosses are also common in Britain: in Scotland and its islands; in the Isle of Man; in the old kingdoms of Northumbria and Mercia, and in a further scatter across the southerly parts of Great Britain. They are an insular phenomenon, not found in continental Europe.

The map distribution partly reflects and partly conceals another kind of distribution. The crosses tend to fall into distinct groups, which are partly local and partly chronological. Their study raises many questions, about dating, about the artistic connections between different areas, about function, about design and meaning. Some of the monuments are quite elaborate, each including a large variety of iconographic themes and decorative motifs. For example, a well known cross like that of Muiredach at Monasterboice provides a wealth of material for the student of art history. It requires very little study of this monument to see that it is closely related, in the style of its ornament and in the techniques of carving and in the choice of scenes from the Scriptures and other details of iconography, to several other high crosses — the Cross of the Scriptures at Clonmacnoise, the Cross of Durrow, the Market Cross at Kells. These are so closely comparable in so many details of style and execution that one is forced to regard them as products of one workshop or mason's yard, if not indeed the work of one master sculptor.

They form a close-knit group, which is not quite to be described as local, since Clonmacnoise and Monasterboice are fairly far apart. However, the distribution is limited to the midlands, and may be regarded as geographically quite restricted. What does this mean? The monasteries at which these surviving examples occur did not belong to a single federation, or 'order'. We may reasonably assume that they were commissioned (probably in the early tenth century, although a somewhat earlier date has been argued) by different abbots, from a craftsman or craftsmen who were themselves operating somewhere within this midland area. How was the job done? Did the sculptor and his helpers carve the crosses in their own work-yard or did they travel from monastery to monastery, staying in each long enough to produce the finished work? There is some little evidence to support the second alternative. At Kells there is an unfinished cross (which is, however, of later date), which suggests that, sometimes at least, the craftsmen worked on or near the site where the monument was to stand. The stone, generally a fine-grained sandstone, was obviously carefully chosen for its purpose and usually brought from some distance away.

These technical questions form one set. There are other sets of questions. How do the crosses of Kells, Monasterboice, Durrow and Clonmacnoise relate, on the one hand to, say, the crosses of the 'Slievenamon group' on the northern slopes of the Suir valley; on the other hand to the crosses of western Scotland? While there are many motifs, and other details, which link them all and show that they belong, as it were, to the one artistic family, it is also easy to distinguish these groups, reasonably sharply.

The Slievenamon crosses, for example, have extremely little figure carving (except on the bases of some of them) but have a wealth of non-representational ornament whose stylistic peculiarities would strongly suggest that they are, broadly, rather earlier in date than the more northerly group. Much of the ornament seems to copy in stone details of ornamental metalwork, suggesting that perhaps the stone crosses of Ahenny, Kilkieran, and other places in south Tipperary and south kilkenny were modelled in part on large wooden crosses sheeted in enamelled and decorative bronze. Possibly large wooden metal-sheeted crosses like this were carried about in procession on ceremonial occasions.

How did such objects turn into teaching or preaching media, which is what the 'Scripture crosses', with their elaborate representations of scenes from the Old and New Testaments and of other Christian motifs would appear to be? How does the evolution of the free-standing cross, as a monumental type, relate to the slab-like monuments of Inishowen, or the slab-reliefs of Pictish Scotland?

Such questions bring us back constantly to a central question. What were the high crosses for, and why are they peculiar to Britain and Ireland? They are not quite confined to the area of the 'Celtic church', since some are found in south-eastern England, but it seems reasonable to infer that they reflect some peculiarity of the organisation of ecclesiastical matters in the far west of Christendom. Perhaps it is that worship in the far west was essentially an open-air matter; that the church building was really not much more than a shelter for the priest and his assistants, the congregation gathering outside in the enclosure-sanctuary, around the symbol of Christianity, the high cross. But this is no more than speculation. Crosses were used for marking the boundaries of the sanctuary area, and also probably as memorials of the dead; but these may have been secondary functions.

But there are also problems which on the face of it would appear to be quite unrelated to peculiarities of ecclesiastical organisation. Why did the art of monumental sculpture die out for some centuries over much of the western Roman world, yet flourish on what would seem to be the barren ground of the non-Roman far west — where it had no good antecedents? This is perhaps the most intriguing of the questions we may ask as we stand in the graveyard at Monasterboice and look up at that astonishing monument in sculptured sandstone which the abbot Muiredach had erected, probably in the first decade of the tenth century. By what strange process was this Roman art transmitted to non-Roman Ireland, to produce major Romanesque momuments at a moment when nothing of the kind was being made in the western lands which had themselves been Roman? It is the mark of the extraordinary vigour of the culture that it can pose such a question: the sculpture tells us more than the chronicles can about its energy and self-confidence.

Something of this ancient self-confidence was glimpsed in the last century, when evidence of the achievements of early Irish civilisation began to come to the surface again, having been all but forgotten. Nationalist Ireland seized eagerly on the evidence as it came to light and wove around it a fantasy of the golden age of the past before the English came.

This fed the many-faceted revival movement of the turn of the century, when efforts were made to recover not only the Irish language but other half-forgotten elements of earlier Irish culture as well. Two movements swept the country, both with considerable revivalist emphasis. One was the G.A.A.: the reorganisation of *Gaelic* games, their conservation and revival in opposition to the games of Anglo-Ireland — rugby, tennis, soccer and so on. The word *Gaelic* became a code-word of the revival, which singled out what was non-English, what related, or was believed to relate, to the time before the twelfth century when Ireland had been independent. The other movement was that of the Gaelic League, an organisation founded in the nineties which became a powerful popular movement at the beginning of the twentieth century. The Gaelic League was primarily concerned with preserving and restoring the Irish language as a spoken language of the people, but, especially in its early days, it concerned itself also with a variety of other aspects of indigenous traditions: it tried to revive the whole of a way of life. People, through these organisations, were encouraged to turn their backs on 'foreign' culture — on the music-halls, sports, theatre, cheap newspapers, jingoism, royalty worship and other manifestations of Britain at the end of the nineteenth century. They were to revive — in truth to invent — their own culture and way of life.

What this produced was, inevitably, an extraordinary *pastiche*, but, in a remarkable fashion, it worked. Tens of thousands attended language classes to learn Irish, and made strenuous efforts to speak the language to one another. The Irish language itself now became a bond which linked 'Irish Irelanders' and excluded others who didn't understand it. The games sponsored by the G.A.A. did in fact become popular and were very soon another bonding agent within the nationalist population. Gatherings of various kinds were arranged, and soon institutionalised, to celebrate the old culture that was being revived, or the new culture that was being invented. People, in cities, towns and countryside, strove to learn the traditional styles of dancing that still survived in many parts of the country, and flocked to attend concerts of Irish music.

One of the oddities of the turn-of-the-century revival movement was the evolution of the form of dress known as 'Irish costume'. This was seen at its most extreme, perhaps, in the attire devised for the theatre, when Celtic-Twilight plays, set in ancient Ireland, were being put on. Cuchulainn and his fellows walked about on the stage in a kind of mini-skirt, showing a large expanse of manly thigh, with triquetra knots and animal-interlace in bright embroidered patches; the hair was bound with a band, sometimes with a curious antiquarian fillet at the front; the calves were tied with criss-crossing thongs; the warrior commonly carried a Bronze-Age leaf-shaped sword and a Bronze-Age round shield. A modification of the costume became associated with 'Irish dancing'. Even odder than this was the cultivation of the saffron kilt as a manifestation of Irishness. The stage costume had some distant relation to past reality, the kilt none.

It is easy to mock all this, as Joyce did, for example, in his portrayals in *Ulysses*. But the movement did transform Ireland for a generation. It also demonstrates that revival never happens. Every culture is unmistakeably of its own period, and if it attempts to restore the past it will produce a travesty. But a travesty is surely valid if it serves the cultural purposes of its time, and in this the Irish Revival movement is no more to be condemned on one level for a failure to restore ancient, or medieval, or early modern Ireland (it's far from clear which, if any, was in mind) than, on another level, the Italian Renaissance is to be condemned for failing to produce the world of classical antiquity.

Early Irish dress, however, is of some interest in itself, if only because there are some oddities about it too. Our information about it is ample but possibly misleading, since the sources for ancient Ireland tend to concentrate on the life and activities of quite a small class of people — those in the upper grades of a markedly stratified society. The chief oddity is that upper-class dress appeared to have departed from the traditional central and northern European style to emulate Roman military garb.

The costume in question was simple, and appears often to have consisted of two garments only, the *brat*, or cloak, and the *léine*, or tunic. the *brat* was a rectangular garment worn over the shoulders and fastened with a pin. It was apparently normally of wool, and dyed a dark or bright colour. It appears usually to have had some special treatment of the hems or margins, and especially of the corners of the cloak. This treatment may have been embroidery, special hem-stitching, or perhaps in some cases even special metal corner-pieces. The *brat* was a long mantle, fastened by a *delg* (pin or brooch) on shoulder or breast, and it could probably be worn in several ways — wrapped closely around the body, worn loosely back from the shoulders, or perhaps gathered or kilted up.

The *léine* was the inner garment worn next the skin. It was probably commonly of linen, unbleached and undyed, and it was a simple frock or tunic. Like the *brat*, it was worn by both men and women. Judging from both descriptions and representations, the *léine* extended to the knee or alternatively to about mid-calf. It was sleeveless, but appears usually to have been gathered in at the waist by a *criss*, or girdle, which was also used for carrying small objects, such as a knife or a purse. It seems that it was common for a hood to be attached to the *léine*. A decorated fringe sometimes, or perhaps usually, adorned the hem of the garment.

It seems that there was a clear distinction between upper-class and lower-class dress in Ireland (not surprisingly) and we have a number of representations of persons wearing breeches, rather baggy in form, which are gathered in below the knee. These would probably represent the ancient tradition in dress. Articles of clothing found in bogs and dating from many centuries later show that in some parts of Ireland at least, at the end of the Middle Ages, men wore plaid trews.

Simple as the aristocratic costume was, it was undoubtedly also elegant, and it lent itself to the kind of rich elaboration which, judging from their metalwork and manuscripts, had a considerable appeal for the early Irish. The somewhat fanciful description of Etain from the old saga, 'The Destruction of Da Derga's Hostel', gives us (in the words of Professor Dillon's translation) an idealised view of the beauty of such dress:

'He saw a woman at the edge of a well, and she had a silver comb with gold ornament. She was washing in a silver basin on which were four birds of gold, and bright little gems of purple carbuncle on the chasing of the basin. She wore a purple cloak of good fleece, held with silver brooches chased with gold, and a smock of green silk with gold embroidery. There were wonderful ornaments of animal design in gold and silver on her breast and shoulders. The sun shone upon her so that men saw the gold gleaming in the sunshine against the green silk. There were two golden tresses on her head, plaited in four, with a ball at the end of every lock. The colour of her hair was like the flower of the iris in summer or like pure gold after it has been polished. She was undoing her hair to wash it so that her hands were out from beneath her dress.'

Such glimpses of Arcady tempted many people who wanted to break out of the shoddy provincialism of late-nineteenth-century Ireland and find their way to a golden past. They didn't reach Arcady but they did go somewhere, and did contrive to sidestep instead of proceeding with Britain into the world promised by the mass culture of industrialisation. The sidestep took them only a little way off the road, but it held, for a generation or two, a sense of community that belonged to an earlier time.

And out of the revival movement came certain achievements. More and more people turned to the Gaeltacht, the parts of the country where Irish was still the native language of the people, and found there a way of life very different from that of ancient Ireland, but very different too from that of most of the modern western world. Three autobiographies, produced in the thirties from the Blasket islands off the Kerry coast (which are now uninhabited) comprise in themselves a remarkable record of an extraordinary survival.

And traditional music survived with the aid of the revival, to be transmitted to new generations and to flourish in the years after the Second World War. Annual festivals of such music, organised in different centres by *Comhaltas Ceoltóiri Éireann*, drew the enthusiastic support of new generations of young people in Ireland, and helped to make certain places in the country pilgrimage centres for young people around the world who were turning to the music of the people. No revivalism is involved: the music is for its own sake and it speaks as much to the future as to the past.

9

IRELAND NOW

In the early 1950s, when I was doing a good deal of field work in various parts of Ireland, I watched in dismay the great exodus of those years. The emigrants left in ones and twos and threes; then, suddenly, in a single season, all the remaining young people would go from a village or district.

This was true even of the east and south, of the pleasant valleys of Barrow and Suir. But in 1956, when for a time I regularly joined the train from the west at Athlone or Ballinasloe on a Friday afternoon, each time there was a coach-load of Irish speakers drowning their sorrows in the bar and emptying the Gaeltacht into the workcamps and industrial towns of Britain. The sorrows, indeed, except for those going to isolated work-camps, were mitigated by then, for sizeable Irish emigrant communities had already built up in the British cities to provide a receptive environment. The emigrants of the 1950s did not travel with quite the same lonely dismay as did many of those who thronged to the factories of war-time England ten or fifteen years earlier when the great migration was in its early stages.

All this has been documented in part. Domhnall Mac Amhlaigh has told vividly about the British end of the process in his *Dialann Deoraí* and John Healy about the Irish end in his *Death of an Irish Town*. The failure marked by this emigration was a very profound one, for the very people who flocked from the country in such numbers were the same, or the daughters and sons of the same, who had fought a revolutionary war in the early part of this century and on whose behalf the revolutionary war had been fought. Their going made nonsense of the official ideology of the 26-county State, of what was taught in the schools and preached from pulpit and platform.

The period after the Second World War saw the breakdown of Northern Ireland, as it had been founded in 1920. As surely, the same period saw the breakdown, or slow failure, of the independent State — a failure at least in terms of the intentions of its founders.

What gradually became clear in that period is that what had come to be thought of as the 'traditional' life of Ireland was coming to an end. This was the frugal, self-sufficient, arcadian rural Ireland that Éamon de Valéra, for example, who was head of government from 1932 to 1948, from 1951 to 1954 and from 1957 to 1959, cherished as an ideal.

This traditional life — the life, very often, remembered by Irish exiles and their immediate descendants – had had quite a brief history. It dated only from the Famine, or just before it. Before that, the tradition was very different, and the work of scholars like Kenneth Connell, George O'Brien and Hugh Brody has helped to demonstrate just how profound the change of the early nineteenth century was. Late marriage, the consolidation of holdings of land, with inheritance by the eldest son, the movement away from co-operation and communal work in favour of household self-sufficiency: these are among the most significant new developments which gave a distinctive character to western rural life of the period from about 1840 to about 1950. The completion of the linguistic change from English to Irish was largely accomplished within that same period.

The influence of developed capitalist society, with its world markets, mobility of people, goods and cultural traits, and tendency to standardisation, has now destroyed the possibility of survival of the traditional culture, and for a long time migration to urban centres has been one of the chief media of transmission of such influence. The moment when emigration ceases to be reluctant — the emigrants being driven out by economic necessity from a valued way of life — and becomes almost eager — the emigrants hastening to a valued culture from one they have come to despise — this moment marks the turning point, and it has long since come to that point over most of western Ireland.

The point of breakdown came, more or less, in the years of the Second World War, in which, of course, Ireland was neutral.

It is clear that the traditional life established after the Famine had many contradictions which weakened its capability of resistance or adaptation to change. Its resilience in spite of these was considerable, but perhaps the sexual isolation imposed by post-Famine marriage patterns on so large a proportion of the population was bound to lead sooner or later to breakdown. At any rate, in the kind of society which was once the paradigm for 'Irishness', demoralisation and breakdown became widespread.

The generation of people who were active and busy with new ideas at the opening of the century tried to give Ireland new directions. These failed, north and south, in spite of strenuous efforts. The economic policy of near-self-sufficiency through protection and import substitution, which was practised from 1932 until 1957, failed to increase the number of jobs, although it had some effect in assisting the migration from country to town. The attempt to revive the Irish language by teaching it to all the children in the schools, which was practised from 1922 until about 1970, failed in its chief aim, although it has some achievement to its credit. The attempt to keep Ireland ideologically and religiously 'pure', sheltered from the ideas and attitudes of the modern world, which was practised virtually from 1922 until 1962 (when Irish television began), failed.

And the failure was recognised, if not fully and openly acknowledged. Another kind of failure was built into the very settlement of 1921, which gave a (then limited) independence to 26 counties of Ireland, and a much more limited autonomy, through 'Home Rule' under Westminster, to the other six.

The roots of the Ulster question go deep, and go a long way back into the past — nearly four hundred years. They are not simple, nor to be explained in over-simplistic terms. There are, for a start, two quite different systems of roots, one deriving from the Plantation of Ulster, the other from the settlement of Antrim and Down. The Plantation of Ulster produced one Ulster problem, the problem of a community divided almost equally, the problem of rural mid-Ulster and of the Plantation towns. In Armagh, Fermanagh, Tyrone and Derry — leaving aside Donegal and Cavan (the other two Plantation counties, now in the Republic) the Ulster problem has been one of fairly equally balanced populations of different origin, half-merging over the years, decades and centuries, but half-keeping to distinct traditions. This problem, had it been isolated, was amenable to the operation of time. The largest Plantation town in the area, the city of Derry, developed in due course into something like a miniature of pre-Treaty Dublin: a city governed by an ascendancy minority but swamped by a majority from the common population of Ireland. Plantation Ulster, in spite of myths to the contrary, could have been as well absorbed into an all-island Ireland as Cork or Mayo, not much less amenable than these to rule from Dublin.

Antrim and Down, on the other hand, saw much more massive immigration across the North Channel, often into areas which had been wholly depopulated. There was, as nowhere else in Ireland, large-scale replacement of one community by another. The growth of Belfast compounded this, since Catholic immigration to the city did not, as in Derry, produce a majority, while Protestant immigration added the frustrations of rural Plantation Ulster to the prejudices of the Irish Scots of Down and Antrim. It is the frontier which runs between the Shankill and Falls Roads in Belfast that was, as it were, extended out into no-man's-land to form the boundary of Northern Ireland, shielding most of those who saw themselves as heirs to the Plantation, in the mid-Ulster counties.

Once the boundary became an 'international' frontier, it began to acquire a deeper reality. The border between Cavan and Fermanagh may once have meant no more than the border between Cavan and Monaghan. But when two separate states came into being, the Border deepened its meaning. Green post-boxes on one side, red on the other, were no more than symbols, all the more so since the ciphers, VR, ER or GR, cast in relief on the boxes in the reigns of Victoria, Edward and George, remained visible under their different pigments.

Time works changes. Those in the border counties on the Free State side who were unhappy at the change were tempted to move into the neighbouring counties on the Northern side. Many on the Northern side (such as schoolteachers who would not take an oath of allegiance to the English king) who were unhappy at being excluded from the independent Irish State, moved the other way across the Border. A pressure, on both sides of the Border, built up against those elements in the population regarded as being untrustworthy in terms of allegiance to the new political systems. As a result, where there had been a gentle gradient, Loyalist-Nationalist, Protestant-Catholic, in the frontier-zones of Ulster, two-way movement of people produced a much sharper divide. The boundary began to appear not as an arbitrary line drawn as a contour on a gradual gradient, but as a discontinuity. Then, social and political changes defined ever more sharply this discontinuity.

Different patterns of subsidy for agriculture, subsidy for public housing, requirements for local government service, and a hundred other matters soon began to alter the physical appearance of the landscapes on different sides of the Border. South of the Border, for example, the revival of Irish became a matter of State policy, taken therefore out of the hands of ordinary people and manifesting itself to them as a matter of compulsion within the school system itself. North of the Border, the revival of Irish remained a matter for voluntary effort on the part of nationalists.

South of the Border, politics became gradually more and more concerned with the problems of economic survival of a small independent State. North of the Border, economic survival continued to depend on the exercise of pressures in Westminster and Whitehall. North of the Border the Second World War happened, south of the Border the 'Emergency'. Over the course of more than sixty years, the Border came to define the difference between two experiences. If, in 1921, the Border was historically unjustified, after the passage of more than threescore years, it is, in one way, historically justified. The Nationalists of the six counties, not to speak of the loyalists, have had an experience quite different from that of the citizens of the Republic. The very great majority of them were born under the Union flag, while the very great majority of citizens of the Republic were born under the Tricolour.

A glance at any history of Ireland from the beginning of the century will show that, from 1920 on, there have been two separate and distinct histories. Not the most ardently nationalist historian can avoid, in his narrative, some bifurcation at 1920.

Both the public policy and the general attitude in the South to the Border, for most of the sixty-odd years, was that it represented unfinished business — the last stage, not yet concluded, in the process of winning

Irish independence from Britain., There was little evidence that either government or people in the South at any period since 1920 was prepared to make sacrifices or a real effort to abolish the Border; there was evidence, however, that they were prepared, more passively and negatively, to decline to recognise the right, either of Great Britain or of the Northern Unionists to maintain the Partition. This, for example, was de Valéra's consistent stand during his long years of government. But, significantly, during the War, he refused Churchill's offer of a united Ireland, tendered as an inducement to the 26 Counties to come in on England's side.

Sporadic IRA campaigns directed against the continued existence of Northern Ireland as a British province received moderately widespread sympathy, or at least tolerance, in the South, on the grounds that, while there might be dispute about timing or means, they were directed towards the right ends.

All this time the Border itself was becoming a more and more solid fact of Irish political, economic, social and cultural geography. Some towns, like Derry, suffered decline for a generation because of the Border; others, like Buncrana or Dundalk, had periods of boom for similar but opposite reasons. Smugglers found an interest which became vested. Manufacturers, sheltered from competition or thwarted in their search for markets, learned to adapt one way or another to the customs boundary.

The road system altered, adapting its development to the special requirements or difficulties of Border crossing. In electoral politics the Border assumed a bizarre significance — being no issue at all in Southern politics, where virtually all parties agreed that they should agree on its abolition (and therefore agreed to forget about it). In the North, on the other hand, all parties agreed that this was the only issue on which elections should be fought. Or, if they felt otherwise, like the Northern Ireland Labour Party, they effectively removed from electoral politics, not the Border issue, but themselves.

Several real attempts — as distinct from rhetorical declarations of intent — have been made to abolish the Irish Border. At the very beginning, a boycott of Northern Irish goods was a pressure directed against the new Unionist administration, and there is evidence that in the first Free State government, Michael Collins, before his death in civil war, may have been contemplating armed intervention in the North, in spite of the Anglo-Irish Treaty. De Valéra's negotiations with Chamberlain, which led to the agreement of 1938, had the Border as an issue, if not the central one. The Mansion House Committee, during the period of the Dublin Inter-Party Government of 1948-51, was an attempt to overthrow the great wall of Ulster by the blowing of public relations trumpets.

Apart from these relatively brief moments, however, the Border has been a centre of paralysis rather than activity in Irish politics, until Seán

Lemass in the sixties began to give it a shade more than *de facto* recognition. By doing so, he was indicating in effect that the Republic could not delay indefinitely the solution of some of its urgent problems on the grounds that the major national question had not yet been settled. He attempted to by-pass the Partition issue.

The Civil Rights movement in Northern Ireland in the late 1960s also attempted to by-pass it, and to deal with some of the urgent internal problems of Northern Ireland without reference to the North-South question. Their failure to do so is bound up with the failure, in the middle term at least, of the Lemass attempt.

The sustained conflict which developed within Northern Ireland from 1969 on, and reached its height in the early 1970s, while it had spillover effects, both in the Republic and in Britain, was on the whole contained within the six counties. It led to the downfall of the Protestant-Unionist home rule government that had subsisted for half a century, and to a return of direct rule from Britain. After one or two unsuccessful experiments, that remains in force at the time of writing, and the problem and the conflict remain unresolved. What a British Minister described (looking at it from a sufficiently safe distance) as 'an acceptable level of violence' was attained, and continues.

The ferocious events of the late sixties produced in the South, first, waves of sympathy for the Northern nationalists, then, with indiscriminate bombing, incomprehension, doubt or distress. The powerfully emotive sacrifice of the IRA and INLA hunger-strikers of 1981, in the Maze prison at Long Kesh, came too late to overcome the revulsion which had affected Southern opinion in respect of the IRA campaigns.

A mental barrier had reinforced the political boundary, as more and more people in the South realised that they had little understanding of Northern problems, and therefore the less sympathy for them. The forces which overthrew Stormont were drawn, in overwhelming proportion, from within Northern Ireland.

Meantime both Ireland and Britain joined the European Economic Community in 1973, and both have been affected in different ways by the world economic crisis which began, more or less, in that year. The Republic, with disastrously high unemployment, and an extremely young, chiefly urban, population in the middle 1980s, faces almost intolerable economic and financial problems. Twenty years of encouraging investment, with huge tax remissions, by foreign and multinational companies, produced, after a period of comparative, but brief affluence, a spreading disaster. Many of the companies pulled out again as the world recession set in, others repatriate most of their profits, the State has borrowed heavily, and a crushing burden of taxation is borne by one part of the (comparatively small) working population, half of whose tax money

Belfast City Hall

Waterford City by night

Du

atrim

The Docks, Galway

St. Patrick's College,
Maynooth, Co. Kildare

Parliament street, in Kilkenny

goes to pay interest on the monies borrowed abroad. This is virtually a Third World problem, and Ireland in the eighties faces the enormous task of re-thinking the meaning of its heritage and the possibilities of its destiny.

Abject poverty was the lot of the greater part of the Irish people for centuries. Misgovernment, or the outlook and attitudes of the governors, must be a major contributing cause. There appears to have been an imbalance between population and the resources available to the population within the existing system which led at one time to an explosive increase in numbers; then at the next stage to a catastrophic fall, followed by steady depopulation. If depopulation ultimately slowed down and ceased, the equilibrium then achieved was precarious, because it depended on the possibility of disposing of any surplus of people which might occur, over and above what the system was geared to support. Economies are man-made.

Emigration is one of the most important facts of Irish life over the past century and a half. Its volume came to be controlled, not by conditions in the countries receiving the emigrants, but by conditions in Ireland.

So, in the 1940s, and again in the 1950s, when the economy was in a bad state, many tens of thousands of Irish people left, mostly for England. When, as in the later 1960s, the economy was in a better state, emigration diminished and the population began to increase. In the twentieth century, as in the nineteenth, developed industrial societies have generated a demand for immigrant labour. At times of rapid expansion, as during the Industrial Revolution in England, or in late-nineteenth-century America, the demand rose largely from the need simply for more and more workers, to build canals, railways, roads, factories, or to man the machines for industrial production. More recently, the demand has appeared to arise partly from the rising expectations of workers in the advanced countries themselves. These workers hoped for better living conditions and were increasingly unwilling to undertake certain menial, laborious, or socially uansatisfactory (not always the worst paid) work. So, for these tasks, Turks, Greeks, Yugoslavs, Portuguese were imported into Germany, for example; and into Britain Irish, Pakistanis and West Indians.

There are many historic precedents for such a development. It is, in some respects, the present-day equivalent of the slave trade of earlier times. Slaves, it is true, were often a source of energy; and in modern advanced societies energy was supplied from other sources through machines. But slaves, historically, have also been employed for other tasks than those concerned merely with the supply and application of energy — for menial tasks or for work which, even if it was light, the slave-owning people were unwilling to do for themselves.

This trade in people, apart from its effect on population levels, cannot have failed to have other effects on Ireland. It may well have helped, for example, to maintain the deep conservatism of Irish society in some areas of life (although this conservatism is offset by a disposition to radical and sudden change in other areas). The society, in spite of rebellions and uprisings, was resistant to some kinds of social, economic and cultural change. In the early part of the twentieth century, when political agitations and parties were numerous, active, and at times violent, Ireland failed to generate any large-scale effective socialist or labour movement. Emigration fell away to a minimum after the beginning of the Great War and didn't resume until a decade or so later. This may be related to the revolutionary activity of that period, although it would be oversimplifying to suggest a straightforward cause-and-effect relationship. But the fact that Irish labour could always find a market abroad, over very long periods, has provided an easement for social and economic pressures building up at home.

Therefore, while fluctuations in the emigration rates have been controlled essentially by the state of affairs within Ireland, this was because the external demand was more or less constant, even if not always in the same place. But there have been times when the external situation could be seen to be the controlling element — notably (in opposite ways) in the time of the two World Wars. But a significant point of change came — it can be precisely dated — in 1973. It is not connected with Ireland's entry into the E.E.C. in that year, but with the oil crisis which introduced a period marked by a changed relationship between the rulers of the developed western world and, on the one hand, the outside world, and, on the other hand, their own labour forces. Widespread unemployment derives partly from rapid structural change in the western economies, partly from deliberate policy, as the rich laager against the poor of the world and strenuously attempt to reverse the long modern drive towards liberty, equality and fraternity. There are few places for the emigrant ships to go, and Ireland is faced with the unprecedented problem of having to absorb its own population increase.

Superficially, Ireland would seem to have been an exploited country in the period when emigration rose to its great heights in the nineteenth century. Emigration itself therefore was long seen as an aspect of exploitation by alien rule, and bringing it to an end has been a declared policy of the independent state since its foundation. There is much substance in this, but the true meaning of emigration is more complex. It can also be seen as a device by which the population of the country was brought down to a level which enabled those who stayed at home to raise *their* living standards (a very inefficient way of doing it, but that is beside the point). It can be seen, in other words, as exploitation of the emigrants not by alien rulers, but by their fellow-countrymen.

It can be seen too as a crude substitute for the contraception which more developed countries use to control their numbers — but this is not a very perceptive view. Or it can be seen as a process which has little to do with exploitation at all; rather a correction of the movements which in early modern times brought large numbers of Irish people into parts of the country which are virtually uninhabitable and caused large numbers to press upon too few resources elsewhere.

The mud cabins of the 1840s in Ireland contained almost no furnishings, and showed no advance, materially, on the conditions of the Neolithic period. Indeed Neolithic people in Ireland probably had more material goods and better equipped houses than the destitute of pre-Famine days who lived at the lower end of the social scale. Today, quite small cottages contain equipment which is fabulously beyond the dreams of affluence of a medieval emperor — television, motor cars, electric lighting and other equipment. Yet it is still — round the globe — a world of mud cabins or their equivalent, and the Irish labourer drinking his tea is drinking the product of an exploitation as bad as that which afflicted his ancestors. He himself, in other words, has joined the possessing, or exploiting, part of the world.

When, faced with calamitous famines and the destruction of the fabric of a traditional society, the mass of people in Ireland in the nineteenth century decided (with however deep regret) to reject much of their heritage, to learn English and to set their feet upon the lowest rung of the ladder which led into the British system with its rewards and hazards, they made a decision more momentous than the vote to join the E.E.C. They voted in effect to share the benefits rather than suffer the exactions of Empire. Part of the price to be paid was emigration. It was painful, but less painful than starving to death within the imperial system. It became less painful still. The benefits of Empire came, and emigration became virtually institutionalised.

Now that has come to an end. The Suez fiasco of 1956 marked the end of an imperial *attitude* which, by and large, not many Irish people had shared (the revival of the attitude in very recent years has no substance to sustain it for very long). The oil crisis of 1973 marked the beginning of the end of an imperial, or post-imperial *situation* whose benefits, such as they were, had been shared to an extent by most Irish people. The world economic crisis which it initiated had long been in the making and seems likely to be only in its early stages. There are limits to growth. The moving frontier eventually comes to a stop. The world is unlikely much longer to be persuaded to owe the West a living, and as more and more factories become idle, the emigrant has nowhere to go.

In the early years of independence Irish governments tried to wall the country off from the outside (western) world. Protective trade barriers, with import substitution, and censorship of various kinds to keep out the thoughts and views of London, Paris, Berlin and New York all failed. Then governments invited the outside (western) world in: hamburgers, pornography and micro-chip factories. This failed too. The most recent governments have given the impression of having no idea what to do next; no idea even of what they would *like* to do. Politicians are held in lower esteem in present-day Ireland than perhaps they ever were.

But the country is not wholly demoralised: it is the people who run it who have lost touch with changing reality. Most of the people who live in it are coping, one way and another, with the changes. There are great structural weaknesses — a badly under-educated middle and managerial class, for example (although its members usually have *training* in various techniques, or 'disciplines', which rapidly go out of date). There is widespread and crippling poverty. But the young people, who form such a large proportion of the present population, are several generations removed from the preoccupations of those who, under British rule or just emerging from it, saw their place in the world very differently. They are, mostly, urban. They share tastes and interests with other young people around the world. They face daunting and depressing prospects if Irish society cannot find a new model. They themselves, however, are the Irish society that must find it. And they display energy and humanity. It is no accident that Bob Geldof comes from their number: young Ireland has been showing for some time that it feels fellowship with the wider world. The mid-eighties are not the best of times in Ireland. But they are by no means the worst.

Dublin airport

Stormont, Belfast

The Dublin Area Rapid Transport (DART), the fast coastline train which links Howth to Bray

Dublin City Carnival, 1985

Royal Academical Institution, Belfast

An Aerial View of St. Patrick's College, Maynooth

Plate Notes

Satellite view of Ireland.
The photograph of Ireland taken from space shows clearly some of the main structural and other physical features of the island: the rim of coastal hills directing drainage inward; the different character of the west; the great variation of landscape through the south-west; the repetition, in miniature, of the features of the island as a whole in Ulster.

Joyce's Tower, Sandycove, Co. Dublin.
The Martello Towers built in the early nineteenth century to defend Ireland's (and other countries') shores against Napoleon's navy, came in later years to various secondary uses. In *Ulysses*, James Joyce commemorates one of these uses — as a lodging for impecunious young men. The tower in question is now a Joyce museum.

Mare and foal at the National Stud.
The National Stud in Co. Kildare is a highly efficient and successful state-sponsored enterprise, engaged in one of Ireland's major export businesses.

Gateway, Guinness's Brewery.
The brewery is a very extensive complex of buildings, centred on James's street in Dublin, and served in the past by a nearby canal terminal, a light railway system, and a fleet of barges on the Liffey. Arthur Guinness in 1759 bought an earlier brewery (Rainsford's). The black brew he and his successors provided became one of Ireland's best known products, at home and abroad.

Ferbane power station, Co. Offaly.
Two of Ireland's chief 'semi-state companies', the Electricity Supply Board and *Bord na Móna* (the peat board), joined to provide electricity through peat-burning power stations, located at the bogs, which were machine-harvested. This has transformed the appearance of many Irish landscapes, especially in parts of the midlands where the great expanses of bog stretch for many miles.

Shannon and Round Tower, Clonmacnoise.
Almost in the exact centre of Ireland, the Shannon winds its way through great expanses of bog and passes through the glacial esker ridge that winds east-west across the breadth of the country. At this point, St. Ciaran in the sixth century founded what was to become the great monastic city of Clonmacnoise. The twelfth-century church of St. Finian, with its attached belfry tower, is one of a number of ecclesiastical ruins that stand on the east bank of the river on the now deserted site.

Skellig monastery.
Early Irish monastic buildings were mostly built of perishable materials such as wood and wattles. But the small monastery (which may have housed about a dozen monks) on the Great Skellig off the coast of Kerry in the Atlantic, was built of stone (without mortar) and still survives. There were six cells and two small oratories.

The Giant's Causeway.
In the Tertiary geological period there was a phase of intensive volcanic activity in the north-east of Ireland, in which basalt poured out in a series of flows to form a great plateau overlying the chalk of earlier times. Along the north coast, at the cliff-like edge of the plateau, the basalt forms a lower layer of regular hexagonal columns and an upper layer of irregular prisms weathered into fantastic shapes. 'Fingal's Cave' across the North Channel in Scotland has corresponding formations. In legend, this 'natural architecture' is said to have been the work of a giant.

Dun Aonghusa, on the cliffs of Inishmore, Aran.
A great cliff-top prehistoric fort, of unknown but possibly Iron Age date. According to medieval legend, ita was built by Aonghus, a chief of a people called the Fir Bolg who were believed to have ruled Ireland in the remote past.

Bourne -Vincent Memorial Park, Killarney.
The demesne of Muckross Abbey, on the shores of Killarney's lakes, amounting to 10,000 acres, was presented to the nation in 1932 by Mr. and Mrs. Bourn and their son-in-law, Senator Arthur Vincent, all of the USA. The park and its gardens are maintained by the Office of Public Works. The park is one of a number of splendid garden-estates, but is probably the most magnificently situated.

Clew Bay, Co. Mayo.
A corridor of the limestones of the central lowlands reaches the west coast here, dividing the metamorphic rocks of west Connacht into two parts. It is covered with drumlins, which form an archipelago as it enters the sea. This bay with its island-swarm appears disproportionately large on many late-medieval maps.

Tomb chamber with carved basin, Knowth, Co. Meath
Professor George Eogan's excavations have revealed two passages, with chambers, under the great Neolithic mound at Knowth, in the Boyne valley near Newgrange. Carved basins have been found in a number of the Boyne tombs, but this one at Knowth is different in being elaborately ornamented.

Ruined megalithic tomb, Carrowmore, Co. Sligo.
The remains of a great megalithic cemetery extend across the coastal area between Sligo town and Knocknarea. The tombs were variants of the passage-grave type and were once covered by round cairns. They have been greatly damaged (and many of them destroyed) by quarrying. Sometimes little more remains than the ring of large stones which once formed a kerb or revetment around the base of the mound.

Stone circle, Athgreany, Co. Wicklow.
Known, like a number of its kind, as 'the Piper's Stones'. The monument consists of a ring of carefully graded great stones, and a separate outlying stone (seen in legendary fancy as a ring of petrified dancers and the piper who played their dance tune). This is a ceremonial or ritual site of the Bronze Age, and is one of many such in the country.

Turoe, Co. Galway: carved stone.
This is a fine specimen of La Tene art, dating from a century or more before the time of Christ. It is one of several in the east Connacht and south Ulster area. They were almost certainly religious monuments of the Celtic lords who seem to have dominated this region for a number of centuries.

Book of Leinster: page.
The Book of Leinster (misnamed) is a late-twelfth-century manuscript, now in the library of Trinity College, Dublin, which contains an important miscellany of materials relating to the history and literature of early Ireland, including a version of the *Táin*.

Air view, Tara.
The earthworks, enclosures and mounds, which extend for about two kilometres along the ridge of Tara, are of different periods from the Neolithic through the Bronze and Iron Ages. They are given fanciful names in medieval myth and legend, which held that Tara from immemorial times was the seat of the rulers of Ireland.

"The mound of the Hostages", Tara, Co. Meath
This mound, fancifully named in the Middle Ages, was excavated by Professor Sean P. O Riordain and Professor Ruaidhri de Valera. It was found to cover a Neolithic megalithic tomb of the passage type. In the earthen covering over this a large number of Bronze Age burials had been inserted.

St. Manchan's shrine, reproduction.
It was a custom in the early church to enshrine relics of holy people, which were then venerated. Many of the reliquaries were small and were 'house-shaped' (actually tomb-shaped, since tombs were frequently made in the form of miniature houses or churches). St. Manchan's shrine is, however, a large reliquary of this form made in the twelfth century. It is of wood covered with cast and jewelled bronze, including a series of human figures which are modelled on North European Crucifix-figures of the period. St. Manchan's shrine is kept in a church at Boher, Co. Offaly, near the church (now ruined) for which it was originally made. The photograph is of a copy of the reliquary housed in the National Museum.

Armagh.
The ecclesiastical capital of Ireland viewed from the main doorway of the Roman Catholic cathedral. On the hill just beyond the town centre, the square tower of the Church of Ireland cathedral rises above the spot where St. Patrick is said to have founded his church in the fifth century and where Brian Boru was buried.

The Great Skellig.
The Armorican system in south-west Ireland produces parallel ridges of Old Red Sandstone, and at the western extremity the valleys between them are drowned by inlets of the ocean. The peninsulas so formed end in rugged cliffs and their line is continued by isolated rocks and islands. The pyramidal Skellig rocks, eight miles off the Iveragh peninsula, are the haunt of tens of thousands of birds. Monks built a small monastery, high on the shoulder of the Great Skellig, probably in the seventh century.

Book of Kells: page.
The minutely and lavishly decorated church manuscripts of early ireland are products of a sensibility remote from our time. The Book of Kells, a Gospel book in the library of Trinity College, Dublin, is the most sumptuous now surviving, although it seems that there were others like it. It has illustrations as well as symbols and formal decorations. The page here reproduced shows the arrest of Christ in the garden of Gethsemane.

Old Abbey Theatre.
The Abbey Theatre, founded in 1904 by Yeats and Lady Gregory, played a remarkable part not only in the Irish literary revival of the turn of the century (of which it was both centre and symbol)'but in the political and cultural life of early twentieth-century Ireland as a whole. In the newly independent Irish Free State, in 1924, it became the first state-subsidized theatre in the English speaking world. Its old home, obtained with the aid of the philanthropic Miss Horniman, was destroyed in an accidental fire, but, after a long interval, it was replaced by a new and much more extensive building.

Fireplace, Florence Court.
Florence Court, Co. Fermanagh, home of the Cole family (Earls of Enniskillen), is a fine representative of the Irish country house of the eighteenth century. Its architect is unknown, but the house is thought to have been built about the early 1760s.

Malton view of Trinity College, Dublin.
The views of Dublin by James Malton show the city at the peak of its late-eighteenth-century development. College Green, where in the Middle Ages there had been a much more extensive 'Hoggen Green', was the hub of the city. Here the Houses of Parliament faced the entrance to Trinity College (the University of Dublin). The College buildings were largely reconstructed, monumentally, in the eighteenth century. The Palladian facade is thought to be to the design of Henry Keane and John Sanderson.

W. B. Yeats by J. B. Yeats.
Yeats's father was a sensitive and perceptive portrait painter; his brother Jack was a painter as is his daughter Ann. The poet worked in a milieu where visual awareness was cultivated and it was a feature of the literary revival of which he was a leading figure that it broadened out from the purely verbal to begin in Ireland a renewal (still far from complete) of all the arts and crafts.

Irish soldiers (Dürer).
From the end of the Middle Ages, for some two centuries or so, Irish soldiers in large numbers served abroad, either as mercenaries or as adherents (after 1691) of the Stuart dynasty which had been overthrown in Britain. The extensive confiscations of land which followed the wars of the sixteenth and seventeenth centuries displaced large numbers of young men belonging to the old Catholic gentry, both Gaelic and Anglo-Irish. Many of them sought service with Catholic princes in Europe.

Irish UN soldiers in the Lebanon.
Ireland, since independence, has consistently supported attempts to achieve collective security through organizations such as the League of Nations, the United Nations, and the associated agencies. The Republic has contributed, and continues to contribute, to UN peace-keeping operations.

The generation of writers that came after the literary renaissance of the turn of the century faced the difficulty not only of anti-climax but also the spiritlessness of the new Ireland. **Seán Ó Faoláin**, steadfastly intellectual in his creativity is one of the small group who bore witness to freedom and went on working himself and encouraging other writers to work in spite of an absurd censorship and of the deadening provincialism of Ireland's two post-partition states.

O'Connell monument, Glasnevin cemetery.
Central Dublin's main thoroughfare is named after Daniel O'Connell, 'the Liberator', and a large sculptural monument to him stands on O'Connell Bridge. He was buried in Prospect Cemetery, Glasnevin, a municipal graveyard which was opened in 1831, ten years before he became Lord Mayor of Dublin. Another monument was erected to him there, a copy of the ecclesiastical round towers of early historic times which had become symbols of past glory for the nationalists of the nineteenth century.

Dublin after the Easter rising, 1916.
Central Dublin underwent several episodes of extensive destruction in the early twentieth century. Parts of it, as shown here, were devastated by British shelling when the Irish Volunteers and the Irish Citizen Army seized and defended buildings at Easter, 1916. Later destruction occurred during the fighting against the British in 1920 and 1921 and in the civil war in 1922.

Statue of Jim Larkin, O'Connell Street, Dublin.
The sculptor Oisin Kelly based his sculptural monument to James Larkin on a famous photograph which showed the labour leader addressing a crowd in 1913. The monument stands in O'Connell Street, Dublin, the scene of dramatic and violent episodes during the 1913 lockout.

Edmund Burke statue, Trinity College.
Burke was educated in Ireland, where he was born, and developed his early literary and political capacity in his days at Trinity College, Dublin. He remained throughout his life closely attached to and interested in the affairs of his family and of his country.

Excavations at Wood Quay, Dublin.
Over a period of many years in the 1960s and 1970s, the National Museum conducted archaeological excavations in the old central areas of medieval Dublin, at High Street, Christ Church Place, and Wood Quay. In the process a great wealth of information was provided on Viking and medieval Dublin, and many tens of thousands of finds were made. Extensive remains of the timber buildings of the Norse city were found, as well as parts of the successive ramparts and walls of the city. Great controversy arose over the Wood Quay site, where it was proposed to build new city offices, but part of the layout of the original Dublin was exposed. Eventually, after court cases, the City Corporation proceeded with its plans to erect the offices.

New Civic Offices, Wood Quay, Dublin.
The architect Sam Stephenson has left his mark on modern central Dublin, through the Central Bank, the new Civic Offices and other major buildings he has designed. Many of these have involved controversy, but none more so than the tower blocks of the Civic Offices, astride the medieval city wall and occupying the site where excavation had exposed the lower parts of timber buildings of the Viking period.

Painting of Joyce in Davy Byrne's.
The pub was Davy Byurne's in Joyce's time and is one of the scenes of *Ulysses*. Subsequent proprietors saw the value of the Joyce connection, and 'Davy Byrne's' the pub has remained.

Statue of G. B. Shaw.
Shaw's statue now stands just outside the entrance to the National Gallery of Ireland, looking benignly on those who go in and out. The royalties from his plays (and notably from 'My Fair Lady', the musical adaptation of 'Pygmalion') have, through his will, contributed handsomely to the Gallery's funds. Although he spent almost all his adult life in England, his attitude towards his native city and country always expressed the quality that was the foundation of his writing — a sane, humane and rational benevolence.

Samuel Beckett.
Beckett's career made him heir both to the Anglo-Irish tradition of the literary revival and to the somewhat different modernism represented by Joyce. In France he developed his own remarkable expression of the modern spirit.

Seamus Heaney is at present the living Irish poet most widely read both at home and abroad. An Ulsterman, he is forced to be aware of conflict, but he tries harder and more successfully than most, without belittling the causes of that conflict, to affirm larger values than those from which it stems. He represents the seriousness as well as the creative power of the generation that made its own revolution, in different ways, in the 1960s.

The Giant's Causeway: detail.
The strange precision and regularity of these rock formations have provided a tourist attraction for two hundred years.

Megalithic burial chamber, Carrowmore, Co. SLigo.
One of the ruined tombs from the great Neolithic cemetery at Carrowmore. Here the cairn has been removed but the central megalithic structure — the burial chamber — remains.

Knocknarea, Co. SLigo.
This hill, on the Atlantic coast near Sligo, which figures in a number of Yeats's poems, is crowned by the huge cairn of a Neolithic passage-grave. The central mound is surrounded by smaller tombs. In early Irish legend the place became associated with the sovereignty-goddess Medb (or Maeve), and the cairn was called '*Mioscán Medba*', 'Maeve's lump'.

The Cross of the Scriptures, Clonmacnoise.
Flann, who stylked himself 'king of Ireland', had this cross erected at the beginning of the tenth century. It is one of a number carved with panels which illustrate Scriptural and other episodes as well as panels of ornament in the distinctive decorative styles also found in metalwork and manuscript painting of the period.

Kildare type St. Brigid's Cross.
St. Brigid's Day, February 1, succeeded one of the main (quarterly) festivals of the pagan Celtic year. The custom was widespread into modern times, of making a stylised cross of rushes or other materials, which was then fixed in a prominent place to invoke St. Brigid's blessing on cattle and farm. There are various local traditional types.

Galway Blazers.
The Gaelic aristocracy and gentry of the Middle Ages, the Hiberno-Norman lords, and in modern times, the Anglo-Irish gentry, shared (like their kind in other countries) an enthusiasm for hunting. Many others in the countryside joined them in this, and the hunt is still a feature of country life in Ireland.

Senior hurling final, Croke Park 1983.
Hurling, the indigenous Irish game, was given a new lease of life with the foundation of the GAA. It and Gaelic football draw support from all the counties of Ireland, and the all-Ireland finals in Croke Park in Dublin are attended by huge crowds.

Steeplechasing, Gowran Park.
Horse-racing has engaged Irish interest and enthusiasm for thousands of years. Here, horses are seen taking the fences in a steeplechase at Gowran Park, in Co. Kilkenny.

Air view, Bob Dylan concert, Slane.
The largest gatherings in late-twentieth-century Ireland occur for pop concerts, for the GAA's all-Ireland football and hurling finals, and, it must be added, for the Pope.

Street stall, Fleadh Cheoil.
The *Fleadh Cheoil*, or festival of traditional music, has become an institution since the 1950s. These gatherings, which attract many thousands to different towns, bring together urban young people and people, young and old, who represent rural traditions. The sudden advent of tens of thousands of people can cause problems to a small town — as also happens with pop festivals — but in the *Fleadh Cheoil* the music, played simultaneously in many pubs, remains at the centre of the event.

Irish inn in the eighteenth century.
In places like this, the Irish-language poets of the eighteenth century met to exchange poems and discuss their trade. The tavern and the inn were important meeting and gathering places for the people of a society whose institutions were in a state of disintegration.

The 'Spaniard' pub, Kinsale, Co. Cork.
The old fishing port of Kinsale is nowadays a resort of those, from the city of Cork and from much farther afield, who enjoy good food and drink. The pubs here cater largely for a visiting trade. But the Irish pub, related to but somewhat different from the English pub, is a major social institution throughout the country, and is most commonly, as in England, a 'local'.

Belfast City Hall.
This large complex, the centre of modern Belfast, was built in 1906 on the site of the White Linen Hall. It may be compared with the London County Council buildings on the south bank of the Thames. It expresses the pride and confidence of turn-of-the-century Belfast, when the city had experienced a century of rapid industrialization and expansion.

Waterford City by night.
Waterford, founded by the seafaring Vikings, was an important port for many centuries. Its river, the Suir, flows into Waterford Harbour, the estuary below the confluence of the Nore and the Barrow, well placed for trade with Bristol and France.

Dunluce Castle, Co. Antrim.
The ruined remains of the strongholds and fortified houses of the medieval gentry and aristocracy are to be seen throughout Ireland. Dunluce was rebuilt a number of times, and the first castle, of about 1300, may have been constructed on the site of an earlier cliff-top fort. It was extensively remodelled in Elizabethan and Jacobean times. It has been besieged and stormed or captured from time to time, and in the seventeenth century, a cliff fall took part of the domestic buildings, along with a number of servants, into the sea.

Docks, Galway.
Galway, founded as an English town, an outpost in the Gaelic west, in the Middle Ages conducted an extensive trade with continental Europe. Now its importance as a port has declined somewhat, but Galway, a university city, is the cultural capital of the west and a gateway to the Irish-speaking areas — including the Aran Islands, which could be reached on the *Naomh Éanna*, shown here.

St Patrick's College, Maynooth, Co, Kildare
The largest Roman Catholic seminary in the British Isles, founded as a Royal College. It became a Pontifical university in 1896 and was attached to the new National University in 1908.

Parliament Street, Kilkenny.
A street very typical of urban Ireland at the beginning of the twentieth century. The concentration of pubs is notable. Across the street was the building (now demolished) where the Confederate Catholics met in the mid-seventeenth century, and formed for some years what was virtually a national (and, by the standards of the time, representative) parliament of Ireland.

Dublin airport.
Aer Lingus, the Irish national airline, operating out of Dublin, Shannon and Cork, is perhaps the chief medium of communication between Ireland and the people of the outside world. It is a 'semi-state' body, one of several established in the 1930s which achieved, initially at any rate, considerable success.

Stormont, Belfast.
With partition, Northern Ireland received its own parliament, and new buildings were in due course erected for it, a gift of the British government. Stormont remains a symbol of the aspirations of Ulster loyalists, although the Northern Ireland parliament in its original form was abolished in 1972.

DART train.
Urbanized Ireland begins to face the problems that have long confronted other countries. A fairly effective commuting system, based on electric tramways, was established in the larger cities at the beginning of the twentieth century, but there has been something of a breakdown in the handling of city transit since the Second World War. The DART is a recent attempt to cope with parts of the problem in Dublin.

Dublin City Carnival, 1985
The streets of Ireland, north and south, have become much more lively with the great social and cultural changes taking place since the Second World War. In this Ireland is in line with other countries of the west.

Royal Belfast Academical Institution.
The 'Inst' is one of Ireland's best known schools. Its buildings, designed by Sir John Soane, were completed in 1814, when Belfast was still a comparatively small mercantile city.

Air View of St Patrick's College, Maynooth
The complex was planned by Pugin but much altered in the nineteenth - and early twentieth-century execution. In the upper part of the photograph may be seen the new buildings, including new residences, associated with the expansion and other changes of the second half of the present century.